"When on the mountain
there is no tiger,
Monkey is King."

"When on the mountain there is no tiger, Monkey is King."

110 two-minute business pearls you won't find anywhere else.

by John Malmo

To Betty. She just knows how to do.

Published by Archer/Malmo, Inc.
Suite 500
65 Union Avenue
Memphis, TN 38103
(901) 523-2000
(901) 523-7654 fax
e-mail: publications@archermalmo.com
www.archermalmo.com

ISBN 0-9744725-0-6
Printed in the United States of America

Acknowledgements

An individual may write a book, but there are many people with whom the author must share any credit.

Not one word herein would have been written had it not been for the late Lionel Linder, editor of The Commercial Appeal, professional newspaperman, friend, and a man of impeccable motives, who made possible my weekly business column that lasted for more than 11 years.

Thanks to Lee Lynch, the only man who could deliver a cappella a treasurer's annual report to the tune of Gilbert & Sullivan's "I Am A Modern Major General," for providing a sparkling foreword without a word wasted.

To Gary Backaus for designing this book's innards, a dirty job that always falls to the top guy in the creative department.

To Richard Williams, a crack young designer, who has forged a talented trio of touch, left and right brain to create a superb jacket design.

To Nancy Stephenson, the most under-employed executive assistant in history, for proof-reading change after change after change.

The greatest gratitude is due the hundreds of clients who entrusted our agency with their resources, and to the hundreds of co-workers who helped us fulfill their expectations, some more than others.

Contents

Foreword

The owner and CEO of an advertising agency has a unique look into corporate cultures, strategies and problems in a wide variety of businesses for prolonged periods of time. Unlike the specialty consultant working on discreet assignments, a good agency can have in-depth relationships for decades.

John Malmo has had both positive and negative experiences with hundreds of clients over his many years. He's seen it all. MBA wunderkinds, inept children of the founder, tyrants, wizards, those driven pathologically to succeed, smart operators and some truly gifted men and women.

I would have saved a lot of money and shed fewer tears had I followed the advice in this easy to read book. Keep writing, John Malmo.

— *Lee Lynch*
Managing Partner, CEO and Founder
Carmichael Lynch, Inc., a 280 person advertising and
public relations agency based in Minneapolis, MN

Introduction

I've been working at one thing or another for 52 years. Most important has been the learning. I have been blessed by association with a hodgepodge of extraordinary individuals from whom I learned many times more about business than I imagined existed.

A guy from Connecticut took me door-to-door in 1951, and in 12 hours taught me how to sell. We were Fuller Brush men. He taught me to watch a professional and do likewise. To learn everything about my products and use my sales materials. To organize tomorrow's business today. The value of free sampling. How to ask only open-ended questions, and how to close a sale.

When my older brother bought a second-hand tractor with a blade and sent me out to grade people's yards, I learned never to promise more than I could deliver.

From Sergeant First Class Troy C. Tippins, I learned that you can't always do things your way. University of the South professor, "Abbo" Martin, taught me that college is about getting an education, not a job. Professor Al Sullivan of Boston University taught me that I should write like people talk.

Don Wilder, editor of *The Quincy Patriot-Ledger*, taught me to ask the right questions, learn the facts and assume nothing. Prescott Low, publisher of the *Patriot-Ledger*, taught me how it makes an employee feel to be treated with respect.

R. Craig Shuptrine of *The Commercial Appeal* taught me that one more re-write always makes it better.

John Cleghorn of Holiday Inns taught me that advertising clients seldom can judge advertising, but they know the difference always between good service and bad. Carl Carson of Carl Carson Car & Truck Rentals showed me the importance of turning over what you don't know how to do to someone who does.

Roger Wright of E.L. Bruce Co. taught me the importance of self-discipline, organizing your work and paying scrupulous attention to details. Harvey Creech, Evan Fellman and John Fleming of Bruce gave me the opportunity to make lots of mistakes.

Ed Lipscomb of the National Cotton Council taught me how to write a speech, and the power of parables.

From Cooper Adams of Gem, Inc., I learned to study the competition, out-prepare them, and how to make money with a small market share.

Jack Talley of Chromcraft, Inc. taught me that sales meetings are show business, and good "theatre" makes a meeting more effective. Tom Rawls, an East Tennessee Terminix licensee, taught me the impact and mathematics of telemarketing.

Clint Thomas of Scott Appliances, the smartest retailer I ever met, taught me that a new level of cream rises to the top of the market every day. Harry Paster of the American Asssociation of Advertising Agencies taught me how to turn revenue into profit.

Stuart Vance of Arnold Industries taught me that small companies must conserve resources, and it's cheaper to ride on the map box of the company 18-wheeler than rent a car.

Will Roach, a North Carolina furniture rep, was the first of many from whom I learned that a company's salesmen often know better what the company's business is than the guys who are running the place.

Ed Bailey of John Malmo Advertising, Inc., showed me that how advertising looks can be as important as what it says. Another former employee, Bob Schiffer (the greatest conceptual advertising thinker with whom I ever worked), taught me that copy and graphics should never be redundant, but that one plus the other should equal three.

Matt Harlib, a former CBS television producer, taught me not to jerk a TV viewer illogically from one situation to another. The legendary Alan Barzman of radio creative and voice-over fame taught me that writing a great radio commercial begins with a great ending in mind.

Al Ries and Jack Trout, the gurus of "Positioning," taught me to trust my marketing instincts.

The president of McDonald's taught me to carry the biggest drum or stay out of the parade. Larry Moh of Universal Furniture taught me how to measure business categories to identify opportunity. From Steve Pond, founder of *FURNITURE/TODAY*, I learned how important it is to know everything about your business and everybody in the category.

My own early failures taught me that advertising must revolve totally around the brand, or the brand is lost and the advertising is worthless. The market taught me that advertising works only when everything else is right with the product or service. That no amount of frequency or level of creativity can make a meaningless message meaningful.

Experience taught me that you have to hire motivated people, because unmotivated people can be motivated externally only for a brief period. To do business only with the guy who can make the decision. That an individual with a passion for his business almost never fails.

From some 500 or more clients in every business category, I learned that every company has only two assets, time and money. The more they're willing to spend of one, the less they have to spend of the other.

My dad taught me that winners work through illness and injury, that honesty comes first and that failure is not an option. My mother taught me that "it's always darkest before the dawn." My wife still is teaching me to try to overcome arrogance.

In 1991, Lionel Linder, editor, gave me the opportunity to write a weekly column about what I've learned for Memphis' daily newspaper, *The Commercial Appeal.* This book is a selection of 110 (slightly edited and/or updated) out of 562 columns.

In most, I tried to use an item of current business news to exemplify a fundamental principle of business that I have learned. Others draw simply on the curbstone knowledge of experience and observation to achieve the same objective.

In the case of the latter, you may judge what I say to be merely my opinions. Indeed, they may be, but they worked for me. Where I have drawn on what I've learned from others, though, I believe firmly that these are demonstrable truths.

You can read any individual topic on a slow "Up" elevator and the entire book on a round-trip flight from Memphis to Phoenix.

PART ONE

MANAGEMENT
Make the right things happen.

When on the mountain there is no tiger, monkey is king.

The late Larry Moh was not your ordinary, everyday, mega-millionaire Chinese businessman.

Larry was educated at Shanghai University and the University of Pennsylvania's Wharton School of Finance. He was not born poor.

In 1970, he owned a tiny wood flooring company in Hong Kong. One day he learned of a major new hotel to be built in Hong Kong. Knowing absolutely nothing about furniture, Larry bid on supplying all the hotel's furniture.

Larry won the bid, made the furniture, and in less than 10 years became the world's largest maker of case goods (bedroom and dining room furniture and occasional tables). Larry's story is fat with valuable business lessons.

What Larry did know about furniture is that it was then a cottage industry with no giant players.

He knew also of thousands of acres of dormant rubber plantations in neighboring Malaysia. Larry wondered if rubber-wood might be good for furniture. It is.

So Larry Moh and his pal, Bob Wo, the largest furniture retailer in Hawaii and a guy who knew something about furniture, went into the furniture making business. They bought cheap the rights to millions of board feet of rubber trees and set up sawmills in the middle of them.

They opened a furniture mill in Singapore. Then another, plus others in Taiwan. Then they set up five assembly plants in the U.S., two in Canada and one in Europe.

Furniture parts were milled in the Far East near the raw material. He was the first to pre-finish the parts, then ship the parts to each assembly plant where as few as 40 moderately skilled workers could assemble $40 million worth of furniture a year.

Larry set up a Far East corporation to make the parts, plus assembly and sales corporations in the U.S., Canada and Europe. He could change parts prices to shift profits back and forth between the Far East, Europe and the U.S. to take advantage of currency fluctuations and taxes.

In the U.S., he hired the best designers, marketers and sales people. After about 15 years of success, Larry cashed in. He and Wo sold Universal Furniture Industries, Inc., which they had taken public, and walked away with nine figures.

Larry bought wood cheaper. He centered manufacturing next to the raw materials. He put the most labor-intensive factories in the middle of the cheapest labor. He shipped cheaply because he shipped only parts. He centered assembly, the least labor intensive, where the highest labor costs existed and close to the biggest consumer markets.

"Of all the businesses in the world that you could have gotten into," I asked Larry, "why did you choose furniture?" Larry smiled. "There is o-o-o-l-d Chinese proverb. When on the mountain there is no tiger, monkey is king."

2 | If knowledge alone were power, librarians would rule the world.

If knowledge or information were power, as goes the saying, librarians would rule the world.

"Information by itself is at the bottom of the (business) food chain," according to Edie Weiner in *Forbes* magazine. "Implementation is power."

Many executives have too much information. One of the reasons management consultants are in such demand is to sift through all the information.

Decisiveness is the most necessary and most lacking executive skill.

American business was thrust into the new millennium at the speed of light. Long-term planning now is 90 days. Short-term is Friday. The ability merely to make decisions has become the hallmark of successful CEOs.

A few years ago, somebody had the guts finally to declare a charge of $50 million and liquidate the remaining assets of Singer's furniture division. Nobody would buy it.

If somebody at Singer had the nerve 10 years earlier to put its furniture division out of its misery, it would have saved Singer stockholders tens of millions.

In the so-called information age, the ability to get information about almost anything was supposed to be the new engine to drive business. And hippos climb trees.

Information is a lot like liver and onions to a 6-year-old. The more you chew it, the bigger it gets. There is so much research data, so much information at the fingertips of most executives, that it is overwhelming.

There are two critical aspects of the job of CEO. First, to decide what the company is or will be, the direction in which he or she will lead the company. The second is the ability and fortitude to make decisions, to be actionable.

The search for decisiveness is one reason why more than a third of the CEOs hired by over 400 major corporations in the 1990s were hired from outside the corporation.

Boards of directors decide increasingly that decisiveness, the linchpin of leadership, is more important in a CEO than company, even category, experience.

When executives get bogged down with information and have difficulty making the right decision, it's usually because they can't identify which of the data are critical. From all of the input, there is always one factor, maybe two, that will play a make-or-break role.

Pick out the make-or-break factor(s). Concentrate on that. Make a decision. Act.

"In 40 hours I shall be in battle, with little information, and on the spur of the moment will have to make most momentous decisions. With God's help *I shall make them* and make them right," said the late Gen. George S. Patton.

3 | Yeah, he has stripes, but can he use a bayonet?

Sergeant First Class Troy C. Tippins was treetop tall with the lean and hungry look of Katie Elder's boys. When he spoke, you thought somebody had yanked a T-bone away from a pit bull.

Sergeant Tippins was pretty sure of his position and authority with 200 raw recruits at Fort Jackson, S.C. He believed that his authority was derived from those five chevrons on his arm and the threats of KP or the stockade.

Little did the good sergeant know.

The fact was that not one of those recruits was very anxious to end up in Korea, but if he did, he darn well wanted SFC Tippins to be at his side.

Most business managers operate from the same point of view as the sarge. They believe that their power is derived from the authority that has been conferred on them by their positions.

"They need to learn that the real source of their power is their own knowledge and skill, and the strength of their own personalities," according to J. Sterling Livingston in a 1971 issue of the *Harvard Business Review*.

Forget the stripes on his arms. Each of the 200 recruits was convinced of Tippins' superior knowledge and skill if it ever came to warfare. To a man, we'd have given 10 to 1 that he could take out single-handedly an entire company of North Koreans.

We respected him for that, not the authority placed in him by Congress.

When business managers can't display the knowledge, skill and experience to justify their authority, everything breaks down. Nothing is shallower or more ineffective than a title without demonstrable justification.

It's become a cliché to point out the important difference between management and leadership. Nonetheless, management is a role conferred from the top. Leadership is embodied in skill, knowledge, experience and personality.

Livingston points out that psychologists determined long ago that people strive for managerial positions not as a need for achievement, but a need for power. It's the reason, he says, why companies fail when they try to turn these hard-chargers into "consultative or participative managers."

Managers or leaders must function in styles dictated by their own unique personalities, not some model defined in the executive suite.

If the justification for a supervisor's role is clear to those being supervised, exercising his or her personality in that role will be the most effective.

If the position is unjustified, even raw recruits will expose the pretender, and no manner of threats will keep the enlisted troops productive.

When the CEO changes his role, the company changes.

When successful businesses begin to falter, often we say that the company has quit doing what made it successful.

If the company achieved success with innovative products or services, perhaps the products are no longer innovative and have not been replaced with others that are. If success came from high quality, we identify a failure to maintain high quality.

In the case of service businesses, it's easy to point to a diminished level of superiority. A company may have loosened the tight financial controls that had made it the lowest-cost provider.

Hardly any company has not gone through a period in which management seeks the reasons for a downturn or flattening out. If the reason is, indeed, a failure to continue doing what it had been doing, it is hard to identify. If identified, it is harder to admit.

When companies quit doing what made them successful, a common reason is that management has changed its role. When it does, that role either goes unfilled or filled by replacements of lower skill, training, experience, creativity or enthusiasm.

When the people who are responsible for business success change their roles and delegate duties that they, themselves, had performed, often success disappears. If they personally had done the selling, they turn it over to someone else. If they personally had created an extraordinary level of productivity or cost efficiency by running the factory, they now spend less time in the factory.

Their new roles usually involve so-called executive duties. But in most companies executive duties are not truly functional.

What made IBM successful was being innovative in computer design. Not manufacturing computers. When IBM was not innovative in computer design for the emerging personal computer market, IBM faltered. It wasn't "IBM" that quit being innovative. In all probability, it was some new person or persons who had taken charge of innovation.

If you examine companies that are continually successful, you find that the people whose performance created that success continue to perform in the same performance areas.

Leaders remain close to the most critical functional roles of a company. When the Indians see a chief function, they follow his lead. The sign above the Infantry Center for budding second lieutenants at Fort Benning is not, "Send Them Into Battle." It is, "Follow Me."

If a chief ceases to be a functionary, somebody else becomes the chief functionary, and it's unlikely that the replacement can match the original.

When the CEO changes his function, he almost certainly changes the company. In a successful company, seldom is that change for the better.

5 | To change the company culture, you must change the company.

Each company creates its own culture, hires people who fit that culture and reinforces it every day.

Once in place, it is difficult to change and almost impossible to get one group of people to act differently. It's hard to change things, a pipe-dream to try to change people.

Employees get on a payroll usually because they reflect existing company culture. There's something that tells the hirer they'll fit in. They act, or learn to act, as they think is expected of them. That behavior is reinforced daily.

Then the company tries to change, so management tells the employees to fit a new mold.

"All of a sudden the same old performance is no longer reinforced, not rewarded. No more chewies," says Gardner Brooksbank, a corporate psychologist. "People react just like laboratory animals. They start the same old routine all over again. They work harder, faster, longer. Still no chewies."

They are obsolete.

Once, 407,000 people took home a Big Blue paycheck. Today it's closer to 200,000. For years, IBM didn't know it needed to change. Then it tried to change everything with the same people. The existing people didn't change things enough or fast enough.

They couldn't.

When the CEO couldn't change the IBM people, finally the board changed him. That worked because the new CEO understood that the same problem existed with the rest of the team.

Even if you could change people, you can't change them fast enough. You need a bunch of different people. For 25 years, IBM developed a corporate culture of managers, not innovators. Even insiders said that when IBM managers faced a problem, they didn't make a decision. They called a meeting. That was the culture.

All businesses today depend on ideas. Resources are heaped on the right idea. IBM no longer had the right idea and you can't expect 400,000 people who were hired, trained and rewarded to manage the old idea to come up with new ideas.

"People don't want to change. They do anything to resist it, and companies don't change until their backs are against the wall," Brooksbank says.

Even if you knew how to change existing people, in a large company you can't communicate the changes. "Imagine trying to communicate quickly through dozens of filters a new corporate culture to 400,000 employees," Brooksbank says.

When companies have pursued the wrong idea for any length of time, better management is not the answer. Better ideas are the solution, and people hired and trained to manage the old idea are not where to look for new ideas.

6 | Stop giving trophies to the losers.

By the end of April 2003, 19 golfers had earned more than $1 million on the PGA Tour. Fewer than half have won a tournament.

A few years ago, British golf pros said that Americans had lost their desire to win. They said American pros become rich on the Tour by losing every week.

There appear always to be enough auto sales to satisfy auto salesmen/women. Otherwise, why can so few of them answer questions about the cars they're supposed to sell? The restaurant business is so good that the owner can walk across a dirty floor to grab a magazine instead of a broom.

Some of us grew up with, "To the winner go the spoils." Too many today grew up with, "You can't win 'em all."

Two or three out of 100 high school students are trying to be class valedictorian. Out of 100 new employees, one or two may aspire to be president of the company.

In children's sports, the winner used to get a trophy. Then the runner-up, then every member of the winning team, then runner-up teammate trophies. Some leagues give everyone in the league a trophy for participating.

We're training Americans to be mediocre, to lose. Today, "To everyone go the spoils," but the spoils have been diminished.

Advertising gives more awards for creativity than there are total employees in all advertising agencies combined. There are so many championships that we have no more champions.

What American business needs is some real champs.

Holiday Inns was not founded to be the best motels in America. McDonald's never was intended to be the best hamburger. Yet Holiday Inns was founded to be the most successful. McDonald's never tries to *beat* the competition. They want 'em out of business, turned into parking lots.

There are many reasons why people lose their passion to be No. 1. Some guy missed the Olympic team a few years ago because he was too arrogant to vault at lower heights for the necessary points, then missed higher. Decades of arrogance turned the U.S. automobile industry into an also-ran.

The need to win is critical to business. As long as we teach kids that they will be rewarded when they lose, losing won't hurt.

Those kids grow into businessmen and women who are satisfied with losing. That diminishes competition, lowers the bar. So we end up with guys making millions running companies into bankruptcy.

To win, hire guys who want your job and don't reward the losers.

7 | Companies must grow just to survive.

Throughout 25 years of growing a service business from zero to $30 million, a friend used to ask regularly, "Why do you work so hard to get bigger? You will just have to work harder."

There are obvious reasons for business growth, such as increasing your income and cushioning the business against a downturn. One not-so-obvious reason is to acquire and retain top personnel.

No business can grow without good people. No business can retain good people unless it grows to create bigger opportunities for those people.

Many years ago, Bank B was No. 2 behind Bank A in a major city. Bank B's CEO went on a recruiting binge. He upped starting salaries and hired a wealth of top young talent coming out of college. He hired more than the bank currently needed and more than existing opportunities could ever hope to satisfy as this talent matured.

Then two things happened. First, the fierce competition between these young bankers propelled Bank B past Bank A. In the 1960s and early 1970s, it was well known that at Bank B you ran fast or you ran last.

Then the largest banks in two other markets became available, and Bank B gobbled up both of them.

Insiders said that one reason the Feds picked Bank B as the acquirer of these two substantial banks was that Bank B possessed a greater depth of young executive talent to manage the acquisitions than did the other bidders.

These acquisitions propelled Bank B into a position as its state's first statewide bank. Even those and other acquisitions by Bank B, though, were not enough to hold onto its entire stable of thoroughbreds. One could hardly read the newspaper without learning of yet another Bank B officer departing to become president of another bank somewhere.

Bank B's CEO understood that a deep bench created victories, and that, in turn, winning was necessary to create playing time for his bench.

Franchise players are rare. When one shows up, you must not turn her or him away. You must not let her go elsewhere. If you have no opening, create one. If you can't meet the payroll with one more body, remove the least of your existing bodies and replace him with a potential star.

Be aware, though, that you must create growth opportunities in the business for these stars, or they will become competitors.

If anyone ever asks why you work so hard to grow your business, just tell her, "To survive."

8 | # Systems are more dependable than people.

The presumption is that you would get better service from Microsoft if you dealt with Bill Gates. That has truth.

No employees work with the same dedication and zeal of the owner. So smart owners devise operating systems that don't depend on widespread employee dedication and zeal.

Most businesses in a category hire from about the same labor pool. McDonald's, Wendy's and Burger King get roughly the same applicants. On balance, McD's used to deliver more consistently because it had better systems or enforced them better.

Establishing effective quality control in people-pursuits is the most difficult element to achieve. In years past, you were less likely to find a dirty McDonald's. "If you have time to lean, you have time to clean" was not just a slogan. It was part of McDonald's system.

Establishing effective operating systems means setting achievable, minimum standards that are adequate to meet a market's demands.

Enemies of effective operating systems are complexity and layering. Working at McD's is hard work, but it is not complicated. That's why it can hire mentally handicapped workers. No McD's employee misunderstands the job. Many people in most companies have no clear description of what they're supposed to be accomplishing.

"Extend the forefinger through the trigger guard, aim at the enemy closest to you and squeeze." That simplicity helped win all this country's wars. "Extend the forefinger through the mustard trigger guard, aim at the patty closest to you and squeeze" has helped make billions of burgers.

The more layers through which operating systems must be communicated, the more complex they become. If you could tell the guy who is going to fry your eggs exactly how you want them, you'd probably get them that way. When a waitress scribbles it and sticks it through a window, the cook interprets, and you get eggs the way he likes eggs.

Advertising agency clients would get better advertising if they dealt directly with the writers and art directors who make the advertising than by dealing with an account executive who must interpret.

You must create a system for employees that is simple enough to overcome such factors as his girlfriend is mad at him or her child's teacher called for a conference.

You have to communicate and enforce constantly through as few layers as possible. Then realize that if you don't get the desired results, you'll have to change the system. It's easier to change a system to fit the people than to change the people to fit a system.

If you can't do that, find a system *you* can work in.

9 | Love thy *good* competitor.

When asked why he didn't attend his industry's trade association meeting, my neighbor, Joe, said, "Why should I want to spend three days at a meeting with all my competitors?"

"They make crappy stuff, sell it too cheap, tell lies about me and my products and try to steal my customers. They're all bastards."

My friend, Jimmy, who's in a different business, said, "I love this business. We have a lot of good competitors. It pays to have good competitors."

Without knowing any of Joe's competitors, it's hard to judge, but he's a smart guy. On the other hand, Jimmy made a terrific point that we often overlook. Good competitors are good for almost every business.

So what's a good competitor?

Virtually all of Jimmy's competitors, at least the major ones, make pretty good quality stuff. They work hard to trade up the consumer into better quality merchandise. His major competitors spend millions of dollars advertising their brands and products to consumers. They help the entire industry by increasing consumer awareness of the category and building the industry's share of consumers' dollars.

Bad competitors are carrion. They are Johnny-come-latelies

who jump into business categories built by others, then bleed the credibility and efficacy of the category for their own benefit. They add nothing. They get in, sell a lot of people once with cheap prices and zero value, then get out.

Of course, there's another type of bad competitor. That's the totally honorable, well-meaning amateur. He's just naive, at best. Stupid, at worst.

He enters a category for which he's unprepared. He eventually goes belly-up, but in the meantime, he screws up a category or market so that nobody else can make a legitimate margin.

This kind of competitor is so numerous in some low-entry-cost categories that the entire category is low margin and unattractive. Travel agencies, bookstores, advertising agencies, shade-tree mechanics are pretty good examples.

Good competitors bring something to the party. In some way, they help enlarge the category to make a bigger or richer pie for everyone. Often they bring innovations that rub off and improve a category, help it grow.

When Domino's went nationwide with home delivery, the pizza business boomed. Domino's added value. Consumers benefited, and competitors benefited by getting slices of a bigger pie.

FedEx didn't put UPS out of business. FedEx created a new, higher-priced, overnight segment of the business that benefited UPS, too, in the long run.

The moral is to love thy good competitor and stay out of categories in which amateurs and predators create perpetual turmoil.

10 | Mismanaging a downward cycle may exclude you from the upward cycle.

Most basic business categories revolve constantly in cycles from hot to cold and back again. There's no greater challenge than operating a business at the bottom of a category cycle.

Every experienced owner and manager knows that when your business category is hot, you're hot, and when it's not, nothing you try seems to make any difference.

If category sales are down 20% or more, as the airline business has been since 9-11, there's little any brand honcho can do to overcome it in the short run.

When the cola market loses its fizz, as in recent years, no growth strategy in the cola war is successful.

The first step is to know if your category is going through a phase of its normal cycle or if the category itself is endangered.

Some of us remember trampoline centers 40 or so years ago. Once that business soured, it went "poof." Are tanning beds a basic category or a fad? Do high-priced coffee houses such as Starbucks have staying power?

Every successful entrepreneur in fad categories is a realist. Her objective is to sell out before the category reaches the top of the bell curve. If your business is in a basic category with historic cycles, the very worst thing to do is sell out at the bottom of a cycle.

About 25 years ago, the owner of Bruce Hardwood Flooring sold the company at an historic low point in the industry's cycle.

The new owner recovered the entire purchase price within a year or two. With each succeeding cycle, the industry has multiplied.

Wood flooring is a basic category. Mistaking cyclical conditions for a structural change in the category cost the seller tens of millions of dollars.

Every executive must learn to identify the cycle phases in his category and try to manage ahead of each phase. He must learn to adjust in such a way in a downturn that he doesn't cripple the brand for the next upturn.

Executives must understand that making deep cuts during a downturn to maintain the profit levels enjoyed during a category growth period can cause severe damage. Profit objectives should be revised to reflect category conditions in a downturn and to protect the brand's structure for the next upturn.

Nothing beats category knowledge when you're trying to define category life and cyclical phases. As in government and politics, studying your business category's past probably is your most valuable tool in predicting the future of the category, as well as that of your brand.

11 | If you don't call them salesmen, don't expect them to sell anything.

An interesting phenomenon of modern business is the growth of what one adept word carpenter calls "creeping meatballism."

It's his definition for the increased lace that is appliquéd to the titles companies bestow on their people. It's turned taxi drivers into transportation specialists, janitors into sanitary engineers.

Consider the lengths to which companies have stretched to keep from calling anybody a salesman.

A recent bit of shirt-tail research into salespeople for radio and television stations, for instance, uncovered 19 different titles. Only five mention selling.

Most are now "account executives." Some are "marketing executives, marketing consultants, media consultants, advertising consultants, customer service representatives, merchandising reps, new business development specialists" and "account supervisors."

Yet the people who bear all these titles have only one job, to sell commercial time on a radio or TV station.

Surely, these titling efforts are not intended to fool the customer. It does not require an advanced degree to know that someone from Station W-whatever is not in your office to consult on brand strategies.

These cloudy new titles must have been created to fool the

title-bearer. If that's the case, these stations must have weekly executives meetings, consultants meetings or specialists meetings. It would expose the charade to invite account executives or marketing consultants to a mere sales meeting.

Most of us assume that titles are to provide at least a slight hint of what a person is supposed to do. A plumber plumbs. A master plumber plumbs masterfully. Who would have the nerve to ask a liquid distribution consultant to crawl under the house to fix a rusty pipe?

Similarly, it would be a contradiction to expect a marketing consultant to ask for an order.

There is one American business category, sports, thankfully, that has changed titles to actually make clearer what each guy does. Instead of a quarterback, for instance, football now has drop-back quarterbacks, roll-out quarterbacks and wishbone quarterbacks.

Basketball now has power forwards, small forwards and wingmen. Even baseball no longer has mere pitchers, but starting pitchers, middle relievers, setup men and closers. That makes sense.

It would be a welcome leap backward if companies awarded titles again that identify to the bearer and recipient of a business card what is the bearer's job. The recipient would know immediately that this is the guy who's going to drive her to the airport, not discuss her company's vehicle fleet requirements.

Odds also are pretty good that a sales force that carries business cards that identify them as salespeople might even sell more.

12 | It's not how brave you are, but how long you're brave.

Following his victory at Waterloo, the victorious Duke of Wellington was asked if his army had been braver than Napoleon's. The Duke replied, "Both armies were brave. Mine was just brave for five minutes longer."

Such is the case in all warfare, sports and business.

Victory goes not, necessarily, to the bravest, strongest, fastest or cleverest. It goes to those who sustain their bravery, strength, pace, dedication or quality for a longer period.

Especially in business, consistency is what separates long-term success from a flash-in-the-pan.

Wellington's army suffered crushing defeats in several skirmishes at Waterloo. The battle was won because the British and their Prussian allies withstood those losses and renewed the battle each time with ferocity.

We all have watched businesses emerge, enjoy meteoric growth, then plateau and slide into obscurity or complete demise.

It is most evident in service businesses. The restaurant business is typical. A restaurant opens with the best fried catfish, the best Italian or Asian food in town.

In the majority of cases, ultimately these restaurants lose their edge. Owners get sloppy, over-confident. They turn them over to managers who have no equity in the business. When finally the doors close, owners are bewildered.

"I make the best fried catfish in town. What happened?"

They once had the best catfish. They are capable still of preparing the best catfish, but they didn't do it every day. They no longer treated each day as opening day. Customers no longer could depend on it being the best.

This doesn't happen just to service businesses. It happens to retailers and manufacturers. Some of the once-greatest names in American retailing no longer exist, and others are on the ropes.

Every manufacturing category has lost companies that once were major brands.

They always have alibis. Their products became obsolete. Population patterns changed. User habits and tastes changed. Companies had inadequate capital. They expanded too fast, or too slow.

In most cases they just lost their edges. Whether it was innovation, better quality, better location, better value or better service, they quit doing that which created their success.

There is no category of business in which competition allows you to slow down, to stop and catch your breath. If you can't maintain your edge consistently, sooner or later you lose.

Remember the two guys being chased by the tiger. One guy said, "I have to rest. We can't (puff, puff) possibly outrun this tiger." The other replied, "I don't have to outrun the tiger. I just have to outrun you."

13 | When you're halfway there, think all the way back to zero.

Organizations are self-perpetuating. They thrive on the organization itself. Protecting and feeding it often takes precedence over accomplishing the goals for which the organization was originally created.

Hear what one Abraham Zaleznik, a Harvard Business School professor of leadership, says on this subject in 1977:

"An organization is a system with a logic of its own, and all the weight of tradition and inertia. The deck is stacked in favor of the tried and proven way of doing things, and against taking risks and striking out in new directions. Ironically, this ethic fosters a bureaucratic culture... "

The professor's words still are timely. They underscore the importance of periodic zero-based thinking for every business organization.

Zero-based thinking refocuses attention on the basic objectives of a company. It examines the structure, people, processes and strategies. It defines modern buzzwords, such as *rightsizing*. It results in companies that eliminate thousands of employees and never skip a beat.

Most companies were created in times that were different from today. Customer environments, competitive and technological environments differed.

Companies that survive adjust to new environments. Sometimes the adjustments are efficient. Often they aren't. They adjust by adding new layers of workers, new offices, new out-of-town branches and hardware of all types.

Such adjustments often create inefficiencies that erode margins. Periodic zero-base rethinking of the entire structure can restore efficiency. Go back to the basic product or service and mentally restructure the organization in light of today's skills, tools, customer and competitive environment.

Say you're running a 20-year-old company with $20 million annual revenue. Knowing what you know today, and with today's revenue, on a blank sheet of paper draw the ideal organization. You're not likely to draw the same organization you're running today. It won't include the mistakes you made during growth.

You would design a streamlined, lean organization for today's business that is capable of the growth you want next year.

Zero-based thinking is not only an opportunity. It's a requirement. Even if your mature competitors don't, the upstarts will. New competitors without your 20 years' baggage will nibble away at you.

There are jobs and job titles in your organization that are either obsolete, or could be combined, at least, thanks to new technology, new skills and smarter or better-trained personnel. There may be an entire layer of supervisors that has become superfluous.

Start thinking all over again the way you did when you started the business. Twenty years experience and a fresh point of view could be unbeatable.

14 | If someone else can knit better, let him stick to your knitting.

One of the expressways to success is to maximize your abilities and assets and minimize your weaknesses.

The smartest companies in the world, for instance, organize their companies around their strengths and avoid their weaknesses.

Some executives apply this principle to their companies. A lot don't. Most individuals don't apply it to their own careers.

A few years ago, Gibson Greetings, Inc. got out of the printing business. It quit printing cards and gift wrap and divested itself of those facilities. For those products, Gibson became only a marketing and distribution company buying its printing from printers.

Gibson is a profitable, nine-figure company that was known as the highest-cost producer in its industry. What the company does best is create products, market and distribute them. So it decided finally to focus its resources on that and quit printing, at which it was not efficient.

Many large companies have followed this trend of becoming less vertical. The purpose is to maximize what they do best and quit doing at all what someone else can do better or, at least, as well at lower cost.

Another has been Sara Lee Corp. It, too, decided it should allow others to manufacture and process some Sara Lee products so that Sara Lee could devote more time doing what it does best, building brands.

"Slaughtering hogs and running knitting machines are businesses of yesterday," then-CEO John Bryan said. Sara Lee no longer devotes energy to be the low-cost producer in those categories. It can select the low-cost producers to make Sara Lee products.

In the last 20 years, the gap has grown huge between what it takes to make pork sausage and underwear and what it takes to create successful sausage and skivvies brands. Sara Lee reorganized around internal strengths that are superior to competition and avoids areas of parity.

You may think it was easy to spot Sara Lee's areas of superiority. Knowing what to do about it was another matter. Imagine the initial reactions of Sara Lee directors and executives when Bryan told them that the only national brand of pork sausage (Jimmy Dean) and leading brands of drawers (Hanes) and ladies pantysox (L'eggs) ought to quit making the stuff.

You may be quite aware of what you do best. Yet do you know what to do with that knowledge, experience, skill or combination thereof?

Everybody is best at something. Identify what that is. Figure out how to maximize your superiority, and then quit wasting your time on what others can do better.

15 | *How* your company talks is as important as what it says.

You learn a great deal about a company by how it talks.

Companies talk all the time. Talk in their advertising. Talk in their correspondence (including E-mail), talk to define their work and label their departments. Talk through their salespeople, at the checkout counter, on invoices, and internally every company has its own, unique vernacular and tone.

With all that palaver, you'd think somebody would take charge of the company voice. The truth is that the CEO defines the company voice by the way he talks and by the attention he pays to the other voices in the company.

Believe it or not, many CEOs never have seen a sample of their companies' invoices. They don't know what their invoices look like, what they say or how they sound. If they did, invoices would be a lot different.

We've all received invoices that seem to bear little resemblance to what we thought we bought. Most medical invoices are a nightmare. Many customers can't figure out what, if anything, they owe.

Companies develop their own techno-speak even if their businesses aren't very technical. Between the acronyms and pet labels, a newcomer has to spend the first few months just learning the lingo.

Lou Gerstner said that in his early days as CEO of IBM,

"I would sit through meetings and frequently have no idea what a presenter was talking about." After stopping them for a "plain-English translation" they got the point, he said.

Most executives have little idea of what their salesmen are saying and not a clue of what's said to customers in a retail checkout line. Much advertising contains embarrassing grammar, and viewers must mute TV spots that are produced at three sound levels above the programming they interrupt.

Every company's tone of voice and voice level reflect immediately the company or brand. No owner or executive should overlook the importance of how the company talks and sounds.

A good start is to use plain English in how a company defines and labels its tasks and work. It's critical to maintain a customer-friendly tone. Customers should understand what you're talking about, what you're selling and for what you're billing them.

Advertising should have a voice level and tone that make people comfortable. That level and tone should be reflected by all employees, at least those who deal with the public. Check grammar. Despite television, there remain people who can tell the difference.

No techno-speak. No yelling. Keep the talk simple and direct, because simple and direct speech is compelling.

| 16 | Before diversifying, you'd better figure out how to clone yourself. |

When most business executives diversify into new categories, they are well aware of the tangible resources that it demands. Yet, it is a rare executive who admits up front the demands that diversification will make on his, and other executives' time. Also the resulting impact on the core business while they are otherwise occupied.

Any diversification takes much more time and attention than an executive has told his board or his investors that it would.

It's not a problem for just small businesses. You'll remember when PepsiCo shunted its restaurant division into a new and separate corporation, and poultry giant, Tyson, sold and/or closed its beef and pork operations. Tyson closed two beef and pork facilities and sold two beef plants to managers.

You don't have to be a Wall Street guru to know that closures and sales to employees usually mean significant balance sheet write-offs. Nowhere on the balance sheet or P&L, though, do they reflect the lost time of top management on Tyson's core poultry business while they were failing with steak and pork chops (and seafood before that).

The PepsiCo spin-off was a much bigger deal. Their restaurant brands, KFC, Pizza Hut and Taco Bell, accounted for $11.3 billion in revenue (about 37% of PepsiCo's total), about 14% of PepsiCo profits.

Since each of these restaurant chains sells an ocean of soda pop, you might have thought this diversification was logical. Nothing could be farther fetched. Restaurants are more capital intensive than soda pop and snack food; they are volatile retail businesses and highly labor intensive, all factors that require different management experience and savvy.

Not measured on PepsiCo's balance sheet or P&L were what the fast food incursion cost PepsiCo in its core soda pop and snack businesses.

Announcements of the spin-off hadn't reached the recycling bin before PepsiCo announced what *The Wall Street Journal* called Pepsi's, "New Battle Plan to Fight Coke." To a meeting of bottlers, PepsiCo announced, "The company's culture of rotating managers from one job to the next had to stop. Pepsi will keep people in place longer so they can make a genuine, measurable impact on the business." The bottlers cheered.

How much better might Pepsi have fared against Coke if pizza and tacos hadn't shared the PepsiCo brain?

Don't be afraid to diversify. Just remember that whatever time you think diversification will take, especially into a new category, should be doubled. It's not bad, either, if the diversification comes with its own crack management team.

17 | Don't keep fixing the same problem. Redesign to eliminate the problem.

German is one tough language. It's full of little syllables that tack onto almost every root word to add meaning.

Take *schreibgefuhl*, which means "The enjoyment, ease and emotion of writing while simultaneously expressing the aesthetic and artistic elements involved with the written word."

That is some efficient word. It takes 20 words of English to define it. If you really want an example of German efficiency, you ought to see what a German pen company, rotring, will do to make a product perfect.

First, you should know that we're talking real ink pens here. The kind in which you put real ink, not ballpoints.

Rotrings, of course, are not cheap pens. In the 1980s, I spotted a rotring for the first time on a trip to Copenhagen and bought it. It was 90 bucks and a superb writing instrument.

After about 10 years, though, the friction-fitting, not screw-on, top had become so loose that it wouldn't stay on the pen. Amortized at about $9 a year, it was discarded.

A few years later, another was acquired, by then $120. Within a couple of years, the top became so loose that the pen kept coming apart when you clipped it into your shirt pocket. Ruined two darn good shirts.

At $60-a-year amortization, it couldn't be discarded. This time, the Internet was available. Sure enough, rotring is there. So you notify the U.S. distributor of the problem and return the pen.

Several days later comes a personal letter. "We always appreciate when consumers take the time to return a product with which they are experiencing a problem. A replacement is being shipped to you under separate cover. Please allow 2-3 weeks for delivery."

Yeah two weeks. The same day the letter was received, the pen arrived.

The point is not that they replaced a defective pen. Or is it that they did it immediately. Other good companies do that.

Testing the new pen was in order. "Snap. Snap. Snap." The top fit more snugly than its predecessors. Wait. What's this? The pen has a new little ball gizmo that the top must depress and snap over to remove or replace.

After more than 20 years, this successful, high-quality, solid steel product design had been re-engineered to keep the top from falling off.

Most companies merely repair or replace returned products. It's cheaper than retooling. Ultimate respect for any brand, though, comes when the product weakness that caused a defect is corrected.

You'd expect that from an outfit dedicated to *schreibgefuhl*.

18 | MBAs can't manage restaurants.

You've heard of Jack Welch and Lou Gerstner. You oughta know Lee Everhart, because she belongs on any list of business people who are the very best at what they do.

Lee's a receptionist.

She treats every caller, every visitor as though he were his company's CEO. She remembers the name that goes with each voice, each face.

The day she showed up, the interviewer recommended her. "She wants the receptionist job, and she says she wants to retire in that job."

She didn't want to get a foot in the door to become a copywriter, an art director or account supervisor. Unlike her six predecessors, she wanted to be the receptionist.

There are key jobs at every level in every company that require professionals. They don't all have big titles. If you can't identify those jobs and find people who want just those jobs, these positions will remain weaknesses forever.

In the 1970s, my agency represented a company that owned 400 restaurants. The president was an MBA, so he placed high value on MBAs. He hired a bunch and put them onto a training ladder to learn the business.

One rung was managing a restaurant. That sounds logical, and in some cases it may have worked. In most, however, the result was lousy restaurants.

You've eaten in enough restaurants to know you don't want to manage one. If you have 500 customers a day and you're open from 7 a.m. until 10 p.m., there are 27 million customer-seconds in the day to make a mistake. People excuse nothing in restaurants. It's hard work and long days.

MBAs did not spend all of that extra dough on an advanced degree to manage a restaurant for even one day. MBAs want to eat in restaurants, not work in the kitchen or mop the floor when somebody doesn't show up.

Unlike Lee Everhart, the MBA doesn't want to do that job.

Restaurant manager is *the* most important job in any restaurant company. You need people who want to run a restaurant. Putting in charge of a million-dollar investment someone who doesn't want to be there is a recipe for disaster.

Who hasn't seen a company promote its best salesman to sales manager only to lose its best salesman and gain a lousy sales manager? More companies succeed with great salesmen and mediocre sales managers than vice versa.

In every company, there's one critical job function on which the entire operation hinges. Fill it with people who want that job. Never turn over your company's most critical job to someone who doesn't want it, even temporarily.

When the number of retailers decreases, category sales decrease.

⑲

When forecasting sales for a new year, manufacturers consider such factors as product introductions, pricing, competitive activity and estimated demand.

Yet another factor may be more important than all others. That is the state of retail distribution in a manufacturer's category. Are there more dealers to sell next year or fewer?

When the number of retail outlets in any category grows, category sales grow. When a category's retail distribution shrinks, category volume shrinks.

If a thousand new furniture stores open, more furniture will be sold. The new stores won't take sales merely from existing stores. The total furniture market will expand.

Likewise, if a thousand furniture stores close, the remaining stores do not divide the volume of the thousand that folded. They may add some business, but the total furniture market will shrink.

There used to be one or two Oriental rug dealers in most cities. Today, 14 are listed in the Memphis Yellow Pages. You can be sure that 14 dealers are not dividing the previous volume of one or two. Americans are buying a lot more Oriental rugs.

Shrinking retail distribution hits manufacturers twice. They lose the business of customers that close, and there's a smaller category nut to share.

This is why, for instance, makers of consumables such as soda pop and snack food expend much of their effort finding new locations for soda pop machines and snack racks. Availability drives consumption.

Pity the manufacturer of a local or regional brand. Not only is retail distribution shrinking in many categories, many surviving independents are being acquired by regional and national retail chains.

In addition, national chains are cutting costs by consolidating buying functions and acquiring more goods in fewer buying offices.

Consider the supermarket business in any major city. When an independent operator is acquired by a national chain, local brands then must sell a chain buyer hundreds of miles away who doesn't live in that market and isn't interested in buying brands for only one or two markets.

If a furniture rep sold a bunch of stuff to a large, local store that goes belly-up, where will he make up that volume? Competitors won't pick up all the volume from the bankrupt store. Less furniture will be sold in the market.

Many factors drive manufactured products volume, but none has a bigger impact than the size and state of retail distribution in the category.

If you sell a local or regional brand, you should be planning what to do as the number of retailers shrinks, and the survivors have to be sold in Bentonville and Cincinnati.

20 | If you want it clean or right, first define *clean* or *right*.

All your life, you've heard that one flub or another was "just a matter of communications." Somebody messed up because they misunderstood, and that was supposed to make it OK.

Early in your career, you thought these breakdowns in communications might go away, at least improve. In saloon lingo, you thought that eventually everyone would know that "shut up" never means "stand up."

To the contrary, it only gets worse.

There remain today great business opportunities awaiting anyone who can communicate effectively the definitions of simple words such as *clean* and *now* to the people who are responsible for cleaning and for doing anything now.

Clean and *now* don't seem to be difficult words. They aren't meant to be comparative or subjective, such as *good* or *quick*. Something is clean or it isn't. You do something now, or now is gone, and you didn't. These are not negotiable word meanings.

With an executive of an upscale hotel chain, we discussed this business of when something is clean and when it isn't. It's a matter of considerable importance to him. He pointed out that clean, without a specific definition, is whatever the cleaner defines as clean.

When a first sergeant inspected an army barracks, there was no misunderstanding of clean. He wore white gloves. They'd better be white when he left. There was no misunderstanding of a properly made bunk. If a quarter didn't bounce two feet off the blanket, you started over.

These aren't matters of insubordination or disobedience. These are matters of definition.

New York's JFK Airport was known to be dirty, shabbily maintained. Schiphol Airport in Amsterdam is known to be immaculate. The folks who run Schiphol were hired by those who run JKF to clean up the latter and keep it that way.

At Schipol, they have a clear definition of clean and are able to communicate that definition to other Dutchmen. First, they had to impart the Dutch definition of clean to Americans. "Oh, you mean you want the basins to be solid white—no spots—all day long? Why didn't you say so?"

If a restaurant chain sends out a bulletin to 400 managers merely to, "Clean up your stores," there will be 400 definitions of a clean store. A guy got the top job in a large municipal park system primarily because his definition of a clean park matched that of the park system's board of directors.

If you want things done your way, define it specifically. Otherwise, you'll get it his way.

21 | Due diligence is a lot more than just weighing the pig.

The simplest definition of due diligence is checking out the pig first to be sure you don't buy a pig in a poke.

That could mean only weighing the pig, determining its age and health before purchase.

Yet due diligence should include ascertaining the cost of maintaining the pig, of processing it into bacon and ham or its resale value, depending on your intentions.

Likewise, due diligence in mergers and acquisitions is not merely assuring that you get the pig for which you pay. You should know also what, how, when and how much it will cost to do with the pig that for which you bought it in the first place.

Most failed corporate mergers and acquisitions rot from lack of due diligence. There's a failure to get adequate, correct information, or to have a lucid and workable plan for life after merger or acquisition.

Take the $103.5 billion union of AOL and Time Warner.

The premerger promise was that strategic alliances could be formed between all of the parts that would create billions of dollars in advertising revenue.

It was the ultimate bundling approach to selling advertising media.

Large advertisers would be enticed, according to *The Wall Street Journal*, "...with the promise of space in Time, Inc. magazines, air time on Turner cable networks, spots on the America Online service and licensing opportunities with Warner Bros. film studio."

This kind of media package looks good on paper. Yet advertisers like flexibility. Most don't hanker to buy one huge package, because such packages include some of what they want a lot and some of what they don't want at all.

In return for giving up flexibility, buyers expect handsome discounts on the pieces they covet.

In this case it meant that executives of some of the individual pieces of AOL-Time Warner would be unhappy. Each would hold that he could sell his medium individually for more than in a smorgasbord.

Gene DeWitt, former CEO of one of the world's largest media buying agencies, told the *Journal*, "The individual operations at AOL-Time Warner have no interest in working with each other, and no one in management has the power to make them."

If you were basing a $103 billion merger on the success of selling packages of the new pieces, minimum due diligence ought to be making certain first that the pieces agree.

Success of any merger depends on an operating plan of the merged pieces. Due diligence includes developing that plan before the merger.

22 | Manufacturers are not— should not—be retailers, too.

Everybody thinks his business category is tough. That's not surprising. Surprising is how many think other categories must be a piece of cake.

Some manufacturers think retailing is easy. So easy that they open their own retail stores.

A few years ago, a close friend in manufacturing bought a factory in Denver and license to make a major brand for a few western states.

A handful of retail stores in Denver was included in the deal. The previous owner couldn't sell independent retailers in Denver, so he'd said, "To hell with 'em," and opened his own stores.

The stores were marginal under the first owner, and my friend who bought the Denver operation never did know what to do with them. Ultimately, he sold the entire shebang, and the buyer sold or closed the Denver retail stores immediately.

Most manufacturers don't belong in retailing. Gateway can make computers, but it can't manage its retail stores.

London Fog, one of the venerable apparel brands in America, filed for Chapter 11 bankruptcy a few years ago. Its first move was to close 110 London Fog retail stores, leaving only so-called "factory outlets," which seem to be the exception to the manufacturer-as-retailer scenario.

In the 1980s, London Fog ranked with Coca-Cola and Marlboro in brand recognition. Ninety-two percent of Americans knew the brand. The company made a lot of blunders in the 1990s. Its full-gainer into retailing was the biggest.

London Fog alienated department stores, which had been the retail foundation of the brand's success.

The London Fog CEO was quoted in *The New York Times*, "We have reassessed this initiative and concluded that we should not be competing directly with our retail partners." Duh.

Successful retailing is as hard and as complex as manufacturing. Most manufacturers who have opened their own retail stores did so only to provide outlets for their factories. That may seem good for the factory, but it's seldom a sound retail strategy.

In the meantime, the manufacturer's other customers turn to other brands that don't own competing stores.

Successful retailing requires solid retail strategies. Unloading the products of an owner's factory is not a good one. Manufacturers may get away with one or two "showplace" stores, as well as a few factory outlets.

As the London Fog CEO said so delicately, though, a national chain of retail stores for your factory brand is an "initiative" any manufacturer should "reassess."

Like, man, unless Chapter 11 is your lucky number don't even think about it.

23 | Business *slanguage* just adds more alligators to the swamp.

Each generation of Americans creates its own slang. Typical was a recent generation's decision that to define something as really good was to say it was "bad."

To sound important, government creates verbs from nouns. We hope that some day politicians will *prioritize finalizing impacting things*. Religion for centuries has found added importance in obfuscation. Take this example from the *Journal of Pastoral Care*:

"And Jesus said unto them, 'Who do you say that I am?' And they replied, 'You are the eschatological manifestation of the ground of our being; the kerygma manifested in conflict and decision in the humanizing process.' And Jesus said, 'What?'"

Slang and convoluted language are rampant in business. They bewilder and sidetrack. Mastering the new talk becomes, in itself, the job for some people.

"What I really like about her," says 26-year-old Michelle to 27-year-old Kevin, referring to 34-year-old Sherry, "is she's a *restructured team player* with a *vision* to *empower re-engineering* the *corporate paradigm*."

Call it business *slanguage*. Such slumber-party, kickypoo talk is a corporate smokescreen.

Downsizing and *restructuring*, of course, are merely modern euphemisms for, "You're fired." *Empowerment* is what survivors of *downsizing* crave in order to prove worthy of survival.

Re-engineering is to corporate strategy what a primer coat of Ralph Lauren blue is to a serious pair of blue jeans. *Corporate visions* are whatever fit on a coffee mug or T-shirt.

Because *corporate mission statements* are written by teams, they usually include nothing that is actionable.

Most fascinating about this new business-speak is that almost all of these words and phrases involve planning. *Visions, re-engineering, restructuring, value chain linkage, paradigms, empowering, mission statements*, etc. are conference room palaver. There's little to suggest moving work forward, being actionable, making something good happen.

A large body of new-age managers believes that being able to talk this talk is important. Learning and using the jargon has become sacred. Yet it obscures real issues, real problems, opportunities, assignments, productive activities and measurement.

It is fad talk that will be replaced by new fad words and phrases that also will die because they add nothing to the language or the work process.

The real issues are always, "What's the problem/opportunity? What are we going to do about it? When? How much will it cost? Who gets fired if it doesn't get done?"

If you want to get from New York to Dallas, you do not have to go linguistically through Los Angeles.

When you decide it's time to go beyond B-school jargon, remember the words of Casey Stengel. "Can anybody here play this game?"

24 | For a real scare, give your employees timesheets.

In 1867, Karl Marx said that an hour's work was the measurement of value. While it's not, necessarily, a true measurement of value, as sure as Friday-is-payday, it's a great measurement of *cost*.

In factories and many service businesses, workers' time is measured to the second-per-unit of production or performance. They don't put those ticking clocks in UPS trucks for nothing.

Yet in most offices, few companies even try to measure productivity, because they're not sure how to do it.

The No. 1 prerequisite to measure productivity is to be able to measure its elements.

In behalf of productivity, profitability, progress, prudence and downright preservation, consider the daily timesheet as a means to measure one critical element.

Timesheets allow you, ultimately, to measure productivity of the company and each individual worker every day. To establish labor costs by task, project and/or customer. To determine current company workload and whether the company is overstaffed or understaffed.

In some personal service businesses, as accounting, law and advertising, in which work is sold by the hour, everyone keeps a daily timesheet. In quarter-hour increments, each person notes his or her activity by job number, task or, at least, by customer.

There are as many arguments against the practice as there are workers. For those who have kept daily timesheets for most of our business lives, the arguments don't stand up.

In most offices, there is no distinction between work (activity) and productivity (achievement). While meetings could be defined as work (activity), meeting time often is unacquainted with productivity (achievement).

Achievement occurs after individuals leave a meeting.

If you don't believe that, ask yourself if you ever said, "I didn't get anything done today. I was in meetings all day."

The mere presence of timesheet discipline can have an enormous effect on productivity without the boss saying a word. Every worker knows immediately that she is accountable for her time and production.

When an employee starts filling out timesheets, he is the very first to know the score. A 5 o'clock timesheet with one legitimate 45-minute entry for the eight-hour day strikes sheer terror in the heart of somebody who wants to keep his job.

Timesheets weed out under-producers, those mountains of activity and molehills of achievement. Timesheets increase self-esteem and self-confidence among the most productive personnel.

Businesses that buy time from their employees and resell it to customers simply could not survive without timesheets. Even though a business may not charge by an hour's work, it's certainly shelling out for it on that basis.

Try daily timesheets in your office for 30 days, even a week. What you learn will amaze you.

PART TWO

PERSONNEL

Identify and keep the 'keepers.'

25 | You can't afford the people you think you *can afford.*

If you grow up at an outfit like FedEx or Procter & Gamble, you get all kinds of executive training.

If, on the other hand, your work history looks like the back of a V8 Juice label, no one taught you how to be the lead dog. Then one day, you open your own business. You're doomed to make every mistake and learn every lesson the hard way. It's this scar tissue that makes the entrepreneurial hide so tough.

Most entrepreneurs make the same personnel mistake. The first time you have to hire somebody, you hire cheap. You're stretched financially, so you hire the people you think you can afford.

A year later you find out you can't afford them. You're working harder with them than you were without them. You're doing your job and theirs. That's why they were affordable.

Then you learn your next personnel lesson. Hiring's a lot easier than firing.

Finally, you realize that the only people you can afford are those you didn't think you could afford. You will not be setting a precedent when you pay one or two of them more than you're making.

Remember, you don't have to do every job. You just have to know who can.

One almost certain road to success is to hire people who are better than you or, at least, potentially better. Owning the business does not, necessarily, make you smarter than everyone else.

If you never hire anybody better than you, the business never gets any better than it was opening day. Bigger, maybe. Not better. If you hire better people, the business gets better.

When you hire smart people, everybody thinks more of you, because they know that smart people won't work for dummies. So customers think it must be a good company if those people want to work there.

Avoid anyone who needs motivation. Hire people who are self-motivated. Personnel motivation begins and ends at hiring.

An ideal mix is folks who are part money-motivated and part motivated by pride. If all they care about is money, they'll move at the first better offer.

If they have great personal pride, money alone won't sway them. Even if they do leave, it's impossible for them to perform poorly even on their last day. You can run off motivated employees, but you can't squash their motivation.

It's hard to find a company full of talented and self-motivated people that failed. A lot of entrepreneurs fail because they aren't willing to hire people they have to pay a lot and then argue with.

Smart people have bigger vocabularies than, "Yes, Sir."

26 | When talent comes knocking, lose the 'No Hiring' sign.

Unlike the New York Yankees, most championship companies are not built on the free-agent labor market. They are built the old-fashioned way, as were the 2002 World Champion Anaheim Angels, from within.

Companies that prosper decade after decade do so because they develop their own leadership talent. Yes, they may dip into the free-agent market for talent in specialized areas from time to time. People at key levels, though, are homegrown.

The companies about which you read delving into the free-agent CEO market usually are in trouble. IBM didn't bring in Lou Gerstner from outside during its heyday. IBM lured Gerstner only after it had gotten itself in big trouble.

Procter & Gamble, GE, FedEx, McDonald's and Coca-Cola are companies that develop the overwhelming majority of their leadership from within.

A recent *Wall Street Journal* report pointed out that the majority of American corporations do not have succession plans below CEO level. Yet short-term, most companies would be hit harder by an unexpected loss of one or more key operating-level executives than by the loss of their CEOs.

In the case of advertising, for instance, loss of a creative director or key account supervisor would be far more damaging in the first six months than loss of the head man or woman.

Every company needs a strong bench. You cannot have too many talented people, and they are very hard to find. Almost impossible to find when you need one in a hurry. That's why you never pass up talent when you spot it, regardless of your current personnel needs.

The time to bring in talented people is when you don't need them. If you wait for an immediate need, they're never around, or they cost twice as much.

When one shows up, hire her. Some may call you Scrooge, but if you can't afford everybody, cut your weakest link. Never fail to grab good talent because you don't need it right now. Make room for good people. Rearrange your hand and discard the least promising cards. Hire on top of existing talent and cut from the bottom up.

A small-town restaurant guy moved his family to the big city in the '50s and applied for a job with a national chain of restaurants. They told him that they weren't hiring. In fact, they were laying off several hundred people.

"Lay off two more and hire me," he said. "I'll do the work of both." He became a key executive and was there for more than 20 years.

27 | Every CEO needs at least one contrary cuss.

In a conversation with an old friend and client for many years, he said, "Every CEO needs a contrarian."

You wouldn't recognize his name right off the bat, and you won't find *contrarian* in many dictionaries.

Gene Cashman ran LeBonheur Children's Medical Center for a couple of decades and deserves much of the credit for building LeBonheur into the No. 1 health services brand in the Mid-South.

A contrarian is just as it sounds. Somebody whose views and opinions are contrary to yours.

Cashman's comment is right on target. Yet there's a lot of evidence that not all CEOs agree. Overconfidence and downright arrogance at the top have been the downfall of more companies than has their competition.

A good contrarian doesn't give you just a different point of view. A real contrarian is a challenger. He'll get in your face and argue. When he thinks so, he'll tell executive royalty that he or she is nuts.

Honest-to-goodness contrarians are mighty hard to find nowadays.

In every company, even small ones, there's usually somebody who'll give the boss a different opinion. Maybe even disagree. Always, though, just up to a point. A true contrarian can't survive very long within the organization.

A true contrarian must be an outsider. A contrarian must be able to survive the finality of a CEO's wrath. He might be one of the company's directors, a lawyer, an advertising agency guy or a consultant. Maybe even the CEO's wife. Never a CEO's husband, if he knows what's good for him.

Anybody who's ever steered the ship knows that it gets pretty lonely. Occasionally, you get an incredible idea. One that's right on the razor's edge. It's either sheer genius or absolutely nuts.

Ask your contrarian.

Many CEOs are so insulated that no heat gets through. It's unlikely that anyone stood very tall against "Chainsaw Al" Dunlap when he was ripping companies apart right and left, right or wrong.

Surrounded by sycophants, a CEO can convince himself that the earth is square. Since there's no place to hide from their decisions, all men and women at the top need a safety net. That's a contrarian's true role.

Legendary CEOs such as Jack Welch of GE were great listeners. Welch had a couple of savvy, outspoken directors who were anything but "yes men."

If his mindset can withstand the withering assault of a dependable contrarian, the boss is probably right. Let's face it. If the contrarian were always right, he'd be CEO. But, of course, that's not his job.

28 | Paying for potential potentially is a disaster.

To make his point that you don't promote workers based on past performance, a *Wall Street Journal* writer quoted poet Carl Sandburg, "The past is a bucket of ashes."

Promotion should not be used as a reward for good performance, according to him. Criteria for promotion should be how you believe the subject is likely to perform in a higher position.

How could one make such a decision without considering past performance of the employee? Consult a poet, perhaps.

That you do not, necessarily, promote the No. 1 salesman to sales manager because he outsold everybody else is a cliché. The two jobs, salesman and sales manager, obviously, are quite different.

That writer's summary, though, that "No manager can do any better than to promote into success, not from it," is likely to be more wordplay than solid philosophy.

If past performance is not to be judged in a promotion decision, the value of performance is diminished.

It does not always follow that "A" students are smarter than "C" students. An "A" grade, though, is some measure of personal discipline, motivation, ambition and maturity. Job performance measures these same traits, plus others that have value in business.

The *Journal* writer's premise gives the wrong signal. It dictates that only potential matters. Yet the sole value of potential is in its application. If not applied, what good is it?

A young advertising copywriter who earned a good salary pleaded for promotion and a raise. He sobbed, actually, that he couldn't make ends meet for his wife and two small children.

His performance justified neither promotion nor more money. He had great talent, much potential, but his work was only satisfactory, not worthy of his talent. He came late, left early and didn't work very hard. Why did he believe he should be promoted?

The copywriter wiped his eyes and said, "I may not have earned more, but if you'll pay me more, I'll work harder to earn it."

That must be what the *Journal* writer means by "promoting into success, not from it."

With the image of the writer's two small children on short rations of Pop Tarts, the employer gave in. Perhaps the lad was worrying so much about his financial plight that it was harming his performance.

That was Friday.

About 10 Monday morning, the writer returned to work. He burst into his employer's office full of enthusiasm and dropped a handful of Polaroids on the desk. "Look. Look. You gotta see the fantastic boat I bought Saturday."

Two years later he was gone. Thirty-five years later he has made no progress.

Christen him the "USS Potential."

29 | To hire innovators, you may have to visit the playground.

It's very hard to grow existing businesses without new products or services.

A study of 200 of the *Fortune* 500 showed that, when adjusted for inflation, mergers and acquisitions, average annual growth over a 10-year period was negative. In another study, performance of all brands in all packaged goods categories declined an average of three-tenths of a share point annually.

Rarely does any brand or category enjoy sustained growth in existing products or services. Without new products, mergers or acquisitions, corporate America would be stagnant.

Since new products and innovations are so critical to business, it's puzzling why so little attention is devoted to these talents when hiring people.

It's a fact that only a handful of men and women thinks originally. Most don't. Creative thinkers are intuitive. They approach matters with different points of view.

Most employers aren't even aware of them when they show themselves. A superstar brand manager from a large food company said about an enormously profitable new product, "I'm not sure who came up with the idea. I guess it was the committee." Wrong.

Committees refine, table, shoot down, applaud, sometimes

ridicule fresh ideas. Committees do not create them. One person had the original idea for that product. The brand manager can't even identify who it was. Shame.

How can he tap that creative resource the next time?

Some basketball coaches say, "We don't recruit to fill specific holes in our lineup. We just try to get the best athletes." In the halcyon days of University of Louisville basketball, Coach Denny Crum had a stable of 6'4"-to-6'6" guys who were great athletes. Those great athletes made great things happen.

Men and women who contribute fresh perspectives are the great *athletes* of business. They need not be great position players, have the prescribed college major, a degree from the "right school" or an MBA.

These aren't scientists or inventors. They are "What if?" thinkers. "What if we put the bank in a supermarket?" "What if we made a bigger tennis racquet?" "What if we put butter in a spray bottle?" It took hundreds of years for a guy to ask, "What if we made a bigger driver?" The golf industry hasn't been the same since.

When our thought processes become mature, we think negatively, defensively, clouded with caveats. One commonality of people who think in fresh, simple terms is that they seem never to grow up. They think as children do, of *possibilities*.

There is no greater corporate asset than a handful of employees that thinks as children.

30 | If you don't fix blame, there'll be more blame to fix.

Errors lose baseball games, and turnovers lose basketball games. So baseball and basketball keep track of errors and turnovers and who made them.

In business, mistakes lose customers and profits. Every business spends money and time to identify, honor and reward people for hitting home runs. That's a solid policy. Despite how mean it may seem, you'd better keep track, too, of errors and who made them.

Failure to fix blame for a mistake simply invites more mistakes. It's common sense that when people don't have to face consequences, bad or good, for their actions, they believe nobody cares. They think that what they do and how they do it is less important.

When other employees see mistakes go unnoticed, they get the wrong messages about the importance of quality and accuracy in their own work.

A live-and-let-live attitude has become increasingly prevalent at every level of business. It's been fostered by a couple of generations that believe they don't have to accept responsibility for their actions. Parents, society, race, economics, gender, whatever is to blame. "Not *me*."

Who's to blame that Orange County, CA went bankrupt? County treasurer, Robert Citron, who invested "dangerously" billions of county dollars, said he wasn't to blame. Said he was duped by Merrill Lynch. The guys at Merrill Lynch said they weren't to blame. Said Citron was plenty savvy enough to know that his derivatives could leave serious powder burns.

Greyhound Corp., according to just about everybody, was the victim of atrocious management decisions that decimated the company. About a costly reservation system blunder, Greyhound CFO, J. Michael Doyle, said, "Ultimately, it was a group decision."

Therein is the root of the problem. "It was a group decision." "It was by consensus of the committee." "The board all thought it was a good idea." "It was a team strategy."

If your programs, plans and strategies are such that responsibility for results at each stage is not established at the engine, don't expect to fix responsibility when the caboose goes by.

As mean-spirited as it may sound, it is important to write into every plan, for everyone to see, the name of the individual who is responsible for each element. Committees and teams are anonymous. If potentially there is anonymity in who will be responsible, you can be sure nobody will accept responsibility if things go sour.

Be sure your box score has a line for home runs and who hit them. It's just as important to have a line for errors and who made them.

31 | The frat house gadfly might outperform the MBA.

Mom and dad wanted you to be a doctor, engineer or go to law school. You did a bob-and-weave through sales management. You were the fraternity social director, knew everybody's name, hometown and favorite beer.

Or maybe you're an ex-jock with four years of football and PE. You're hot on the job market.

Enterprise Rent-A-Car has built the largest car rental business in America by segmenting the resident customer market and segmenting the bottom half, academically, of college graduates.

Originally, Enterprise shunned high-priced, highly competitive airport locations, and went after the resident market through auto service departments, body shops and insurance companies. For referrals, auto service managers can expect complimentary donuts or pizza periodically from their neighborhood Enterprise manager. It's the sort of thing that endears one to his fraternity brothers.

The company's concentration on a plentiful, overlooked segment of the labor market demonstrates an understanding of exactly the type of guy that Enterprise needs to make its business click.

Most Enterprise hirees hung around corporate waiting rooms competing with MBAs, 4.0 guys and ex-coeds. They networked their moms' and dads' friends, and their moms and dads were right.

The job market is unforgiving of their four-year pursuit of fun and popularity. So the $30,000 job at Enterprise looks like a P&G brand management track.

They work long hours, wash cars, shuttle cars around and spend a lot of time with customers. Raises are tied to the branch profit or a promotion.

Enterprise wants the most popular guy from the frat house. He makes friends quickly at service and body shops. He has a college degree, can talk intelligently and be polite to customers. From ex-jocks, Enterprise gets guys who have spent their young lives competing. They want to win.

Up top, Enterprise may need a few folks who aced calculus. The operating end of the car rental business, though, ain't cerebral. The ex-fraternity social chairman has proven "most likely to succeed."

Enterprise is not unique. Other savvy companies have learned to develop hiring criteria other than just the top 10% of graduates. Many employers, though, still assume that a 4.0 and a graduate degree guarantee better results, regardless of the job.

This is not to trash graduates who made toast out of academics. They're always in demand. It simply demonstrates how the labor market can be segmented as successfully and as profitably as can the customer market.

If the primary needs of the job call for a good ol' boy or girl, a Phi Beta Kappa may not be qualified.

32 | You can teach a lot of things. Personality isn't one of them.

If you observe the human race long enough, you realize that some people are just naturally nice, friendly folks, and some others are just plain ornery.

Some people, for instance, will smile and say, "Good morning, welcome to McDonald's. May I take your order please?" They'll say it every time with a smile and mean it.

Others just flat aren't going to say it, or, if they do, will do more harm than good.

It's not hard to figure out that some people are perfect to deal with the public because they make people feel good. Some aren't. If that's so easy to understand, how come so many employers who hire people to deal with the public don't hire primarily on personality?

They tie up millions of dollars in a store or restaurant. They spend millions more to attract customers, then confront them with a sourpuss.

Another professor has written another article about how management should train employees. Good stuff, too. Don Schultz from Northwestern says management has to, "Help employees understand why being customer-focused is important. Why delivering on the brand promise is important."

Everything the professor says is right. The trouble is that

everything he writes is 100% dependent upon the attitude and personality of the employee. With, or without, his advice, any employee with a friendly, pleasant, outgoing personality makes good things happen with customers.

To a self-absorbed or downright unpleasant bloke, you might as well flush the prof's words down the toilet. Knowledge and training are worthless with a, what-are-you-doing-here? personality.

You can teach almost anybody everything they need to know about your business, your products, policies and objectives. But you can't teach somebody to be nice. If an employee has to deal with customers, and unless your business requires some special technical background, personality should be your first hiring priority.

There used to be a young woman in the marketing department of a savings and loan. She worked in an office all day with one or two co-workers. What a waste.

Her smile stretched from Maine to Los Angeles, and when she laughed the sun shone. She belonged in a branch or on the street dealing with customers. Better yet, she belonged in the personnel department looking for clones.

People like to do business where employees make them feel good, feel important. They don't come back where they don't appear to be wanted.

If your first priority in hiring people to meet the public is not personality, what in the world is more important?

33 | Only revolutionaries
make real changes.

If you're looking for someone to shake up your business, say your inventory or shipping processes, or to create new sales strategies, to whom do you turn?

Absolutely not the guys who shook it up last time and created the current processes and strategies. They'll be too busy defending their decisions in the last revolution.

To create meaningful changes in the organization, you need people who can go on the offensive for change, not defenders of the status quo.

In most companies, though, it is the very people who created the last changes who have earned the reputation as innovative thinkers and are most likely to be assigned the next upheaval.

Instead, you should be looking for a new, probably younger, team of corporate revolutionaries that has seen the weaknesses in existing systems and is chomping at the bit.

This is hardly a new theory of management-sponsored change. It was espoused by Maxwell Hunter, II in the *Harvard Business Review* in 1969.

Hunter likened the concept to the teachings of that true revolutionary, Vladimir Lenin.

"One of [Lenin's] basic premises was that, while a hard core of inner-party members (i.e. top management) must run the system, most of the fighting will be done by the local militia."

"After a successful revolution, the power of the militia leaders must, consequently, be liquidated immediately, before they get any bright ideas about the future."

The moral, according to Hunter, is self-evident.

"If an organization is really going to be in the forefront with respect to technological progress, it must figuratively shoot the leaders of each successive revolution the morning after their great triumph."

With the lightning speed of technological advances on many fronts and the fact that your current systems are probably twice as old as you perceive, most companies would benefit from revolution in many basic operating tenets.

Thus, whom management selects to drive these changes is critical.

It's easy to argue that veterans of the current systems are most likely to be aware of the weaknesses. That may be true, but it is these very people on whom change will land hardest.

Rather, it is bright newcomers, especially those with some experience in other systems, who already are aware of weaknesses. It is these who are less committed to current systems and will have the least to lose when they are changed.

Find your revolutionaries among the bright youngsters who are at the battlefront daily. Afterwards, remember Lenin's advice and don't wait too long to pull the trigger.

34 | Just exactly when is the right time to fire somebody?

Virtually everybody who ever made a payroll knows what is the toughest problem that you ever have to face. It's not the loss of your biggest customer, not a recession, not even an IRS audit.

It's figuring out the right time to fire somebody.

The best answer was attributed many years ago to the legendary Abe Plough, founder of Plough, Inc. His advice: "The first time it ever crosses your mind."

If the thought ever occurs to you that somebody might need to be fired, sooner or later you will fire that person, Plough believed. The sooner the better. If you put it off, several things happen, all bad. The longer you wait, the longer the company suffers the mis-actions or inaction of the employee.

If it has occurred to you to fire an individual, that individual's career is nose-to-nose with a brick wall at your place. He or she has no more future in your company. He or she knows it. So the lives of both you and the employee will be miserable until the axe falls.

The most humane thing to do is to cut the cord today and get it over. The employee will find another job. Whatever that job is and wherever it is will be better for the employee. He gets a new start, a better environment for him than at your place. Most of us who have been fired at least once learn from it, and we end up better for it.

These are all points that many business leaders have learned, but still most procrastinate. The other consequence of delay is the effect that procrastination has on the other employees.

If you think somebody needs firing, everybody else in the place knows, too, that she does. The others become unhappy if you don't get it done. They resent whatever that employee is doing or not doing to have earned firing.

It causes the rest of the folks to lose confidence in the procrastinator. Your capacity for leadership is questioned. You don't know it, but the underperformer is undermining your authority and your effectiveness as boss.

It's important for everybody to know that you have tried corrective action, that you've been fair. Most important is for them to know that you have taken action.

Amazing, too, is how accurate the principle is if you are an unhappy employee. If it ever has occurred to you to quit, sooner or later you will. It works both ways. Just be sure you have another job first.

PART THREE

RETAIL
Nobody else thinks like a retailer.

35 | If you don't like show business, get out of retailing.

Most local retailers do everything they can to keep from being different. Yet creating an identifiable and memorable persona is critical for small retailers, and being different is the quickest way to do it.

Local retailers who are the most successful at differentiation are those who make spectacles of their businesses.

One Memphis retailer, Royal Furniture, used a goofy, sub-human, something-or-other on television called "Jolly Royal." Another put every family member on TV at one time or another in everything from boxing trunks to turkey feathers.

Another retailer, who started business on $5,000, in fewer than 15 years had $18 million cash to invest in a Hollywood movie. He's outrageous, stays open 24 hours a day, walks around in an American flag sport shirt.

He's on television constantly with the same message day in, day out. "Gallery Furniture will save you money." Sometimes he just stands there on TV and throws money in the air. His credit manager walks around the store dressed like a mattress, wearing an Uncle Sam hat.

Wendy's founder, Dave Thomas, had more impact on television for Wendy's franchisees than anything his advertising people had done since "Where's the beef?" Thomas was a tad silly, a lot corny and *effective.*

America likes corn. Americans are, basically, unsophisticated. Strictly defined, to be sophisticated is "to be deprived of genuineness, to be artificial." Thus, to be unsophisticated is to be genuine, *not* artificial.

That's why these retailers were able to differentiate their businesses so effectively. Americans trust corn and its lack of sophistication and guile. We trust people who don't take themselves too seriously to wear some silly getup and tell us how much they want our business.

Like it or not, retailing is show business. Retailers with a good script, who act out that script daily, attract more attention, more customers, more success.

Upper-end retailers have to appeal to a smaller percentage of the market that is sophisticated. The principle of a need to differentiate, though, remains the same. Instead of a clown suit, a Mercedes dealer might differentiate himself by wearing white tie and tails.

Retailers must create a brand personality all their own that is different from the competition. Then they should put it on stage, treat it as though it were *My Fair Lady.* Run it forever. Even if the cast changes, the script should remain the same.

Remember the cliché: *"If you appeal to the masses, you'll eat with the classes. Appeal to the classes, and you'll eat with the masses."*

Smart retailers are like Eskimo dogs.

Eskimo sled dogs cluster into a furry wad to share body heat when the temperature drops to 40-below. The most successful retailers cluster their stores to share management, distribution and advertising costs.

Unless a retailer is highly specialized, distribution is critical for success.

In every major market, successful retailers as McDonald's, Taco Bell, KFC, Walgreens, Kroger have dozens of stores. They cover every inch of their markets.

Yet hope springs eternal in the entrepreneurial breast, and almost weekly otherwise smart guys build one or two me-too stores in a major market and stand at the bottom of a hill they can't climb.

A fundamental of retailing is the ability to spend enough on the brand to buy an adequate share of the retail category's promotional voice in the market. Share of voice leads directly to share of consumer awareness, which leads to market share.

Even brands that are successful in other markets with dozens of stores occasionally try to move into new markets with one or two. They seldom succeed.

When McDonald's opens one new store in any major market, that single, new hamburger stand opens with the benefit of millions of dollars of advertising. With the best possible purchasing agreements with vendors, employee training, management supervision, real estate research, lowest sign costs and legal help.

Blockbuster Video stores built out their markets early with an adequate number of stores to advertise. Mom and Pop video rental stores that got there first were plowed under. Make no mistake. The McDonald's, Blockbusters and Walgreens don't want to compete. They want their competition *out of business.*

Hancock Fabrics is a successful chain of retail fabric stores headquartered in Tupelo, MS. When they had 459 stores, the chairman's letter to stockholders said, "We continue to expand existing markets where the economies of shared advertising, distribution and management are greatest."

Owning the territory with a massive presence isn't just a retail rule. It applies to most competitive business categories. In 1955, Anheuser-Busch introduced Busch Bavarian Beer.

Busch was one of the first brands in America for which geographic distributor selection was based not on state lines but on television markets. Thus, every market that had Busch on the shelves had Busch advertising, but not one Busch promotional dollar fell on an ear without Busch distribution.

In almost every business category, critical-mass distribution, product availability, store clustering are key elements for success. Remember the Eskimo sled dogs.

Remember, too, that only when a brand has adequate distribution in a market can it bark loud enough and hunt in a pack, as hounds.

37 | A good retail buyer has more impact on sales than do retail salesmen.

It's common to assume when business is good or bad in a retail store that the credit or the blame should go to the salespeople or the store's advertising.

Actually, in many retail categories, the credit or blame for sales results rests more often than not on a store's buyers. The people who buy the merchandise to stock any store determine greatly the store's customer appeal.

Even veteran buyers might be surprised to hear, "Your number one job is to attract customers." Nevertheless, that's their job.

After location, the two internal factors that affect sales the greatest are the selection of merchandise in the store and how it is priced. These two elements are influenced most by the buyer.

The buyer selects the merchandise, which brands, the number of brands, styles, colors and sizes. The buyer negotiates the cost, which is the major factor in determining the retail price.

If you go in a store and don't see anything you want, it's the buyer's fault. If it's higher priced than what you've seen elsewhere, that, too, may be the buyer's fault.

It's no job for amateurs.

It's also another reason why so many owner-operated stores are successful. The owner runs the store and makes many sales herself.

She takes her firsthand sales knowledge with her on buying trips, and she knows how much she can pay, because she knows how much she can, and must, charge.

In retail categories such as clothing, home furnishings, gifts and accessories, buying is the most critical job in the store. There are hundreds of resources in each category that make much the same merchandise with much the same costs. Most are brands unknown to consumers.

Successful buyers know how to mix branded and no-name merchandise to appeal to consumers. They learn which vendors can be relied upon to deliver on time and which can't.

These buyers know which brands that, when put on sale, will draw customers to the store and which won't, at any price. They know which unbranded merchandise can be sold at higher margins, because consumers can't compare prices. They know which brands draw traffic.

Supermarkets learned that they can make more money on store brands, but a loss-leader price on Kroger Ketchup won't draw the shoppers that will a low price on Heinz Ketchup.

Brand X Recliners for $149 sounds good. They won't attract the crowd that will La-Z-Boys at $179.

In retail, you can trade two good salespeople and a utility infielder for one good buyer and come out way ahead.

38 | When the neighborhood changes, you'd better change neighborhoods.

Most businessmen and women have heard at least once that their success will depend, sooner or later, on their ability to manage change.

Say you're in the retail business. You sell shoes or cakes or pizzas, laundering and dry cleaning, whatever. Sales have peaked and begun to slide. It's harder every month to make last year's numbers. Things have changed. The landscape has changed.

New streets and new residential neighborhoods are built every year. Zoning changes. Other businesses relocate from old to new locations, in or out of the neighborhood. These factors change population numbers, demographics and traffic patterns.

If you draw your customers from a limited radius of your store(s), as do most retailers, you're in big trouble. This kind of change is gradual, seldom dramatic, hard to spot.

Location often is the last thing that retailers look at when business starts to slide. You think about advertising, pricing, merchandise—everything but location. Destination businesses often survive these shifts, but destination businesses are rare.

Stores have growth cycles from Day One. Similarly, virtually all retail locations peak and mature. Ultimately, almost all follow some bell-shaped curve. What hastens the backside of the curve is when competition is smarter and stays geographically relevant to the market.

The businesses that suffer this kind of slow sales erosion are often small chains, decisions for which are made outside their retail markets. The people who can make decisions about store relocation and new store development come to town periodically and spend their time in their own stores. They rivet their attention to store operations. They don't have a clue what's happening in the city.

The real estate guy at headquarters says his job is taking care of existing real estate and leases. The operations manager that comes into the market says operation of existing stores is her job.

It's the marketing director's job, but nobody told him. All he has to do is know whether customers come from a radius around the store or whether they're intercepted going by the store. He has to watch annual sales records for each store since its opening or the last 10 years, and he has to understand how the market is evolving.

Few stores continue building retail sales indefinitely from the same base in a market. Stores mature. Before changing advertising again and store managers for the seventh time, retailers need to think about changing addresses. That has to be somebody's job.

The first truism is that the landscape is always changing. The second is that somebody has to know it's his job to be the "lookout."

39 | Mom and Pop flourish because they add value.

There are 10 times more supermarket bakeries today than 25 years ago, and supermarket fresh meat cases are five times bigger. You'd think independent bakeries and butcher shops are faltering.

Independents aren't merely surviving. They're thriving.

"I've been here since '82, and we've never had a slowdown," says Chuck Hogan, son of the founder of Charlie's Meat Market. "Our retail business grows every year."

In 1976, there were 2,500 bakery departments in U.S. supermarkets. In 2001 there were 29,800. In the same period, the number of independent bakeries grew from about 17,000 to 24,000. Independent bakeries are growing at the rate of 1,500 to 2,000 a year, according to the publisher of *Modern Baking* magazine.

How do these independent butchers and bakeries flourish in the face of huge supermarket economies and store traffic?

"Experience, quality and service," says Charlie's Chuck. "Supermarket meat departments do a good job, but most of the meat comes to the store already prepared. There aren't many real meat cutters in supermarkets anymore."

Indeed, a customer can select whatever kind of meat she wants in a supermarket or a butcher shop. At a butcher shop, though, she can choose exactly how she wants it cut and approve it before it's packaged.

If you've ever tried to grill three steaks of different thickness, or thicker on one end than the other, you know the problem.

The difference in a supermarket bakery and an independent is even greater. Since most supermarket bakery products are baked off-premises, they can't be as fresh and aren't likely to be as tasty.

To offset lower traffic than supermarkets, the independent bakery enjoys a higher spending customer.

The average ticket in an independent bakery is $8.18. That's 174% higher than the supermarket's $2.98 bakery check average, according to *Modern Baking*. An independent bakery is a destination. The bakery department in a supermarket is not.

Chuck Hogan says he believes he could open more successful meat markets in his market and towns nearby. "The problem is finding experienced meat cutters and store managers," he says.

Huge chain-store brands such as Wal-Mart, Kmart, Target, Kroger, Albertson's and Walgreens will reach almost $400 billion in sales this year. Regardless of how large that figure becomes, chains will never eliminate good, independent, specialty operators.

Smart entrepreneurs aren't merely good butchers or bakers. They know how to compete by finding ways to add value that earn higher sales tickets and margins than chains.

Independent owners who don't survive will be those who try to operate like supermarkets.

40 | Extending service hours works only if you maintain the service level.

For centuries, one of the most successful ways to increase business has been to extend your line.

Henry sold more Fords when he offered more colors than black. His heirs sold more Fords when they offered models other than just A and T. Then they sold more cars called Mercury and Lincoln.

As long as they stay close to categories they know, manufacturers have been able to extend their lines, grow their businesses with great success.

Retailing and service categories also have enjoyed remarkable success from line extension. The Midas Muffler Man is now the "Midas Muffler, Brakes and Shock Absorbers Man."

Some other types of retail and service extensions are harder to accomplish than adding services, menu items or products to be sold under the same brand.

These are extending the number of retail or service locations and extending hours of operation. Restaurants probably are the best example of failure to extend one good location into more. For every McDonald's, there've been a dozen failures to multiply one good restaurant into many.

You might think that a no-brainer is extending service hours under the same roof. Not necessarily so.

A manufacturer's line-extension risks spreading the same number of sales over more individual products. If you're selling 100 black ones and you add red, yellow and green and still only sell 100, you've drastically reduced profit.

It is possible also to dilute the same sales volume of an eight-hour day over 10 hours. Since labor is such a high cost factor in service businesses, this can absolutely devastate a bottom line.

It seems logical that if you extend hours to make it more convenient to do business with you that you will benefit. That may be true, but only if your service quality and productivity do not suffer as a result. If you spread the same employees too thin, or operate with less-qualified employees part of the day, service quality and productivity will decline.

A person is more productive, more accurate in the first few hours of the day. If the day is extended, you will provide a service by employees who are in the least effective part of the day. They will be less courteous, less efficient, less productive, less everything that matters.

You might gain an immediate sales increase, but it may not last. If the service to customers suffers demonstrably, you may even find yourself doing less business in a longer day or week.

In no case, can you extend success unless whatever it was that created the success remains constant.

41 | Retail ad dollars may be spent more wisely on real estate.

Of all the factors that make a retailer successful in any category, none is more important than location.

During their growth, two superstore categories, books and office products, fought a turf war. Barnes & Noble battled with Borders for real estate, and Office Max fought the merger of Staples and Office Depot.

During the heat of battle, Barnes & Noble and Borders had about 700 stores between them. Industry experts said there was room for 800 more. At one point, Barnes & Noble bought up leases on stores vacated by a former home furnishings chain in New York not for its own use, but to keep Borders from getting them.

At the same time, there were about 1,500 office products superstores, and experts said that number could almost double. Staples had a dilemma. After their merger, they had many locations with duplicate stores. If they closed some, they ran the risk of Office Max grabbing the leases.

Gas station, auto dealer, drugstore, supermarket and fast food brands have understood the critical nature of location for decades. It's a fundamental lesson that many entrepreneurs overlook.

Often, small retailers judge a location on its traffic count. Yet regardless of the number of cars that pass a location, some areas are a no-man's land. In every city, you see locations that look good, but over the years, one business after another goes broke at those locations.

The chairman of a sizable bank was furious at his subordinates when they bought a piece of property for a new branch in a growing area. They could have bought the corner lot, but to save $50,000, they bought the property on the side street, 100 yards off the main drag.

"For annualized savings of a couple thousand dollars a year, we have a branch that will never perform to the level it would have on the corner."

Occasionally, location is not critical. Most florists do the majority of their business on the phone. With a few exceptions, it's unnecessary to pay for higher-priced real estate for a flower shop.

For most, though, the right location has more impact on success than any other factor. More money for the right real estate is worth a lot more than twice that amount in advertising to try to draw people to a secondary location.

It's critical to know people's buying habits by retail category. You need to know if more will buy what you sell if you're close to their homes or where they work. Then don't even blink. Get the best location.

42 | For your business sign, look to the 17th Century.

Even all of today's bells-and-whistles technology pales in comparison to one 17th Century communications medium. Namely, trade signs.

A trade sign visually depicts in picture and/or shape the nature of the business operating beneath the sign. More often than not, it is suspended in front of the place of business at a 90-degree angle to the building.

Centuries ago, every locksmith's sign was shaped like a key. Every blacksmith hung out a sign in the shape of a horseshoe. Clockmakers put clocks out front, an optometrist a huge pair of spectacles, a cobbler a giant shoe, etc.

Historians say that trade signs were used in earlier centuries, because a large part of the population was illiterate; couldn't read their own names.

Antique trade signs have become collectors' items, and can sell for thousands of dollars. Many a modern fern bar is decorated with trade sign reproductions.

Modern merchants would be wise to reintroduce the trade sign. Even for the majority of Americans who can read, a trade sign communicates more quickly. There are so many signs on virtually every commercial roadway and at shopping centers that it's hard to pick out individual word signs at 40 miles per hour.

The problem is compounded, of course, by municipal sign ordinances, shopping center and mall regulations that prohibit such simple, clear depictions. Merchants try to solve the problem by substituting well-known logos for graphic symbols of their trades. Two golden arches, at any driving speed, look more like a hamburger than does a hamburger.

That's fine if you have 20,000 pairs of golden arches and hundreds of millions of advertising dollars. A dentist, though, might well be advised to hang a large white molar in front of his office. He'd surely be the easiest-to-find dentist in town.

An Earl's Hot Biscuits restaurant sign was a woman and a rolling pin in animated neon that moved back and forth over a flat hunk of dough. Clearly, Earl stood out from breakfast competition.

Poole Mobile Homes mounted one on a platform about 50 feet in the air. Did anybody other than Poole sell mobile homes?

Specialty retail stores need all the help they can get to build traffic. Cute logos or clever shop names, the interpretations of which are known only to the proprietors, aren't much help. A big pair of specs, a book, a flower, mobile home in the sky, whatever it is you do beneath it graphically depicted on a sign, will stop more people than anything else.

Beats a thousand words, they say.

PART FOUR

RESEARCH
*Good intelligence is
the foundation for good results.*

43 | Don't make quantitative assumptions on qualitative data.

If you want to learn the Bible-buying habits of bifocaled, red headed preachers with congregations larger than 200, you can do it. Today, there is almost no business question too obscure to find the answer.

Research is available to any business, no matter how small. The Internet has made a wealth of *secondary* research available and made even *primary* research more affordable.

Secondary research is that which has been conducted by somebody else, or is gleaned from secondary resources. It's available at the library, from trade associations, trade magazines and, of course, on the Internet.

Virtually, every industry's leading trade journal conducts research on its category annually. If you have an advertising agency that belongs to the American Association of Advertising Agencies, it has free access to AAAAs Member Information Service that has information on all industries.

Primary research is that which you conduct yourself or have conducted on your behalf. It falls, basically, into two categories, *qualitative* and *quantitative*. Everybody's heard of focus groups in which 10 or 12 folks gather in a room to answer questions and express opinions.

They can be very effective, but focus groups are qualitative. You can't project statistically the group's answers or opinions.

Just because seven out of 10 people in a focus group say they like your new red package design better than the green one does not mean that 70% of the split-pea market likes red better. The essential use of qualitative research is to tell you which are the right questions to ask quantitatively.

Knowing the right questions to ask is critical. A well-conducted focus group answers the question, "What is important?" Quantitative research answers which of the things they say are important is the *most important* and to what degree.

The size of the quantitative research sample varies with the size of the market.

Quantitative research costs more because you have to poll a lot more people. Most research buyers pay too much because they ask too many questions to which they don't need the answers.

The best quantitative research is conducted in person or by telephone. Mail surveys are less accurate because they are skewed by the bias factor of who will, and who won't, fill out a questionnaire.

Most people get into trouble buying research because they don't buy both qualitative and quantitative. They try to skip the focus group or to use it for quantitative results.

Those bifocaled, red headed preachers probably want Bibles with big type and they don't want Jesus' quotes in red because red's harder to read than black. But what do we know? They may want the Bible on tape.

| **Unless you can do something with the answer, don't ask the question.**

Modern research techniques have become one of today's most valuable business tools. Once its goodness was discovered, though, there's been a load of money wasted on research.

The primary reason is that research buyers aren't as good at buying as researchers are at researching.

One problem revolves around research that is not actionable. Interesting, perhaps, but not something with which you can do anything. Un-actionable research occurs almost always because the buyer doesn't determine on the front end what he really needs to know. So needless questions are asked that cloud the results or render them worthless.

If you ask needless questions, you get needless answers.

Effective, actionable research begins with a list of decisions that the research buyer will have to make from the research. Then she must ask herself to what questions she needs the answers to make those decisions. Then, she gives those questions, in writing, to the research outfit. When she gets the first pass at the questionnaire, the next step is easy and critical.

She must project every reasonable answer to each question. Then she must ask herself, "OK, if that's the answer, what decision do I make?" If she can't make a decision on any answer that might result, she doesn't need to ask the question.

This does three things. It shortens the questionnaire and reduces the cost of the research. You get only answers on which you can act. It eliminates the need for a second, even third wave of research.

It's not unusual for some research to create more questions than answers

The one certain thing about all research is that it is not cheap. One company of close acquaintance spent $500,000 to learn the market potential of its product. The report was 15 inches thick. Nobody in authority would take the time to read it.

All of the data were the result of a premise that there might be one of the company's products sold per household. It turned out that people bought as many as seven per household.

Research also can be a great smoke screen. A favorite trick of corporate resume builders is to avoid any decision for which the results can be blamed on him. So he buys waves of research in the belief that sooner or later the research will make the decision for him.

Research doesn't make decisions. People do, and if people can't make the decision after one wave of research, they probably asked the wrong questions.

If you don't know what you'd do with the answer, don't pay to ask the question.

45 | To find new products, find out how they use the old ones.

Almost every company conducts market research periodically. Yet many fail to maximize the benefits of their research because they don't ask the right questions, or they don't spend enough time considering the implications of the answers.

On the surface, it may seem silly, for instance, to ask customers how they use your product. To the contrary, the answers to that question can lead to expanded uses, line extensions and totally new product development.

The vast majority of Arm & Hammer Baking Soda isn't used for baking. It's for eliminating refrigerator odors, toothpaste and underarm deodorant. The average wife/mother probably couldn't use a box a year if she used it only for baking.

Why did it take Arm & Hammer 100 years to make toothpaste? For 100 years, millions of Americans brushed with baking soda from the kitchen. If Arm & Hammer had known how customers used baking soda, it wouldn't have taken a century.

Corning Consumer Products Co. has made Pyrex glass cooking bowls for as long as you've been alive.

For several years, the company had conducted a semi-annual survey among primary users of housewares, women aged 20 and older. Its surveys measured everything from brand awareness and advertising effectiveness to customer satisfaction, and how they used Corning.

Lo and behold, they discovered that, in addition to cooking in the stuff, 50% said they used their Pyrex dish-pots to transport food to events such as covered dish suppers and tailgate parties. Bingo.

Many focus groups, vendor sessions, product design, color, packaging and advertising, marketing, pricing, manufacturing and sales meetings later, Pyrex Portables were born. Immediately, Pyrex Portables was a hugely successful new product category.

The product was such a home run that many of the 50 women who were given the prototypes for 12 weeks of testing didn't want to give them back when the tests were over.

Corning let the customers tell them what sizes they wanted, what colors, even what kind of packaging. (Boxes, so they would be easy to wrap for gifts.)

Almost anyone could have told Corning for decades about nightmares of spilling casseroles on car seats if only they had asked, or watched.

If you're already conducting research, you may benefit from spending more time reading the answers. If you're not asking respondents how they use your product category, you should. Every great new product comes from a need of which users are aware.

Discovering peripheral ways in which people use your product may lead you to discover opportunities in your category of which you weren't aware.

46 | New product failure begins with poor research.

Ask guys if they wash their hands before leaving the restroom. Ninety percent say "Yes." Station a spy in the men's room. Probably less than 50% actually wash.

Asking people about their habits is a dicy way to get accurate data. Most researchers know that you have to observe what people actually do.

That said, how does a sophisticated marketer such as Kimberly-Clark Corp. foul up introduction of the first moist toilet paper?

Kimberly-Clark made three basic mistakes. First, it went forward after 63% of adults told researchers that they already moisten toilet paper before using, or they use a premoistened wipe. Uh huh.

Then, according to *The Wall Street Journal*, Kimberly-Clark spent $100 million to develop the roll/dispenser unit. A starter kit of Cottonelle Fresh Rollwipes is $8.99, including the gizmo that goes on your toilet paper spindle and is about twice normal size.

Another $35 million went for test market advertising.

Kimberly-Clark's second mistake was approving the advertising its agency created. As so much of today's advertising, it dances around the product and never gets to the point.

TV commercials show people splashing around in water. In

print advertising a Sumo wrestler moons readers and the line is, "Sometimes wetter is better."

Last, Kimberly-Clark didn't saturate the test area with free samples for people to try the product without blowing almost $10.

A recent study by NFO WorldGroup, a major marketing research outfit, reveals that 69% of respondents purchased some product they didn't normally use after trying a free sample. When the sample included a coupon, 74% bought it.

So, Kimberly-Clark has a new product that consumers probably must change their current habits to use, but research tells them that the majority won't have to change.

The product is tough to demonstrate, so the advertising is cute and beats around the bush. They don't distribute free samples and coupons, though research indicates that three out of four people might purchase if they like the sample and get a coupon.

After a year, Cottonelle Fresh Rollwipes were still in the test region only, and CEO Tom Falk said, "It's going to grow slower than we thought."

If Kimberly-Clark had thought, the advertising would have told consumers flat-out what is the product, and to watch for their free samples with coupons. But it all begins with research.

If people must change their habits to use your product, you'd better know it up front, and people don't always tell the truth. Especially about the bathroom.

47 | ## Testing is worthless if you don't know the reason for the result.

Testing and measuring is a never-ending process in business. You're always testing a new concept, a new product, new offer, new promotion or advertising strategy. At least you should be.

When testing anything, it is critical that you keep in mind what it is you're testing, and that you create every surrounding element to the optimum. If every element is not optimized, and it fails, you will never know for sure why.

Would it have succeeded in a better location? With a better package? With more advertising? With a better test market sample?

Obviously, you have to compute basic costs, selling price and margin, because success for an unprofitable concept or product is not worth much to anybody.

Being too conservative in the testing, though, or trying to test more than one thing at a time will result in no answer or the wrong answer to the original question.

Dobbs Houses wanted to find out if a no-strings-attached, money-back guarantee would fill one of its restaurants in Lexington, KY. They saturated the market with radio advertising for the offer. Customer counts soared.

Thirty days later, they cut advertising in half, and customer counts continued climbing. Thirty days later, they cut advertising in half again. Customer counts leveled off.

Thirty days later, they cut advertising in half again (12.5% of the original level), and customer counts dropped. They returned advertising to the previous month's level (25% of the original), and customer counts returned to their peak. They maintained that level and made out like a bandit.

The original test was to determine if, at any cost, the guarantee would work. Once they learned it worked, they tested how much they had to spend on advertising to make it work before moving to other markets.

If they had begun testing the guarantee at the low advertising level it would not have worked. They would have ditched a successful concept.

It is impossible to test successfully more than one variable at a time. You cannot measure probable success of a new product or concept at the same time you're trying to measure other factors. You will never know which one had an impact on the result and to what extent.

To find out if the dogs'll eat it, you have to remove all other variables, and make sure it gets in front of enough dogs. Don't try to test at the same time three package designs.

The worst possible result of any test is not knowing why you got the result you did.

PART FIVE

PRODUCTS
But will the dogs eat it?

48 | Find a problem. Solve it. Make it proprietary.

American manufacturers introduce thousands of "new" products each year. You'd assume there is a bunch of Rube Goldberg inventors tunneled away in laboratories.

Not so. Most new products do not come out of laboratories. They come from marketing departments.

You can count on your fingers the number of breakthrough products that are introduced every decade. The overwhelming majority can be defined as a "new" raisin bran. It has 26 more raisins.

What's really a new product? The first microwave oven, first frozen orange juice. What's not new is 26 more raisins or orange juice in a new container size.

New products fall into three categories. The first of its kind. Then, there's the same old stuff in a new container, a new size or something added, as a Hershey's Kiss with an almond. Last, is existing technology applied in a new way to an existing product.

Firsts are few and far between. Most are in the second, "value-added," category. It's here also that 99% of new product failures occur. The true benefit is for the maker, not the consumer.

It is the last category that creates most of today's stars. Applying old technology in a new way to existing products costs much less than primary research and the success rate is greater than the "value-added" category.

A textbook example is WD-40. There was nothing new about oil or aerosol spray technology, but nobody had put the two together.

First comes awareness of a need. There are many places you can't reach with an oil can. Then comes the marriage. Thin the oil, and put it in an aerosol can.

The genius was naming it WD 40, not Smith's Spray Oil.

WD-40 is magic. It is proprietary, not generic. Smith's Spray Oil has no magic. Soon, there would have been Jones Spray Oil. Prices and profits would have fallen. The proprietary magic creates the profit.

There was genius in Thompson's Water Seal. It enjoys great success still. Yet now there are many knock-off products.

Velcro is magic. It is not new technology. It is two erose plastic surfaces that stick together like cockleburs. Old technology applied to solve old problems differently.

Velcro remains magic. Joe's Plastic Grippers would have paved the way for competition from Bill's Plastic Grippers.

Find an existing customer need or shortcoming that is common among products in your category. Investigate available technology outside your own category.

When you find the right match of need and technology, make sure to build in the magic, and avoid generic labeling that invites competition.

| ## New product opportunities may be right under your nose.

You've probably agreed at some time that "the grass is greener on the other side of the fence."

Actually, the cliché is, "The grass *looks* greener..."

That's a tremendous difference, especially when it comes to new product development. McDonald's, for instance, in its new product efforts, assumes, apparently, that the grass really is greener over the fence.

Most of McD's new products have come from other food categories. Namely, its efforts to introduce fried chicken, pizza, pasta, carrot sticks, barbecue, corn on the cob, fajitas and such. All outsiders. None successful.

This looking through the fence has produced no new product home runs for McDonald's since Chicken McNuggets more than 20 years ago and salads over 10 years ago.

Yet during these years when McD's was trying everything else, others grew an entire new, and successful, category out of one of the most basic products on McDonald's menu boards.

Coffee.

While McDonald's and most other fast food giants were casting for new products, the coffee bar category has grown to nearly 20,000 retail outlets.

Starbucks, the high-profile leader, has opened thousands of stores and is doing coffee business at the rate of more than $200 million a month.

How could the savvy fast food giants with all their resources overlook such an opportunity for a higher-margin product that was already on their menus? Easy. The bigger you are, the farther you cast your line. Opportunities under your nose go unseen.

You say this is not a fair comparison, You say there's no way that a hamburger joint could have taken advantage of the Starbucks opportunity. You say McDonald's couldn't attract the $2-to-$5 Starbucks Coffee drinking Calvin Klein set.

Well, not every existing fast food chain overlooked coffee. In 1996, Dunkin' Donuts added several blends of fresh-brewed coffee in its stores at prices well below Starbucks, but well above what the donut boys had been getting for a cup of java.

Previously dormant Dunkin' Donut sales shot up 10% overnight, and continued growing. If you can sell designer coffee at the donut shop, surely you can sell it at Egg McMuffin stands.

The most successful new product opportunity very well may be in an existing product or service in your line. Look no farther than the end of your nose.

It's great to be far-sighted, but when it comes to new products, it can be a distinct advantage first to be near-sighted. Look at your own category, your own product line before looking over the fence.

50 | # A breakthrough product is life-changing.

One guy had a walking cane with a spike in the end to keep you from slipping on ice. Another visualized companies paying him to supply on-the-job massages for employees.

For 40 years they've come with biscuits and barbecue sauces, cookies and potato chips, Rube Goldberg mop designs, camping stools, gimmick golf clubs and an electric fishing motor you steer with your foot.

Hope breeds eternally in the innovative American breast and woe is the bloke with a bucket of cold water.

Nothing is so cherished as the new product or new business idea by the person who hatched it and nothing so reviled as reality.

So with all the cocked hats out there, is it possible to spot the one in 10,000 new ideas that might break through?

Two professors in France, W. Chan Kim and Renee Mauborgne, say you can, and they wrote an article on how to identify a winning idea a year or so ago in the *Harvard Business Review*.

They even have the obligatory charts (ugh) to go with it, including a 36-box "Buyer Utility Map" on which you measure "Six Stages of the Buyer Experience Cycle" horizontally against "Six Utility Levers" vertically.

The chart's about as helpful as a compass and flashlight to a blind man, and the authors are quite lucid in Monday-morning-quarterbacking several famous successes and failures.

Nonetheless, they include some useful thoughts for the business innovator.

Among these is the point that, "How a product is developed (is) less a function of its technological possibilities and more a function of its utility to customers." In other words, forget all the techie blarney. What will the idea do for folks?

The aforementioned fishing motor steered by foot, for instance, was a bonanza because it changed the way guys fish. Now they can put both hands on the rod instead of one on the motor.

Not one angler gives a rat's fanny how it did it or why.

That exhibits another of the authors' points, that a new product should offer exceptional utility at an affordable price and a handsome profit.

Bottom line is that most successful new products change consumers' lives in that pursuit in which the new product is used. A new cooking gizmo ought to change the user's "cooking life" (i.e. the microwave oven); a new fishing gimmick, a man's "fishing life."

You get the point.

Some of us got an Acura, because it has radio controls on the steering wheel and that changes your "driving life." Could even save your life.

51 | If it won't save them time, you might be wasting your time.

"Watch this," he said as he opened the glass door of the horizontal metal box and thrust in a stale donut as hard as your Latin teacher's heart.

He punched a button. The box "whirrred" for 30 seconds. He re-opened the door and gingerly removed a piping hot, squishy, donut. "It's an Amana Radar Range," retail appliance guru Clint Thomas proudly announced in 1969. "It's gonna revolutionize cooking."

Microwave ovens are as common in American households today as worn-out mattresses, but they never did revolutionize cooking.

In most homes, microwaves are a high-priced popcorn popper, a leftovers warmer-upper and OK for some food processed expressly for microwaves. Only about 20% of home-cooked meals come out of a microwave.

Microwaves cook nothing better. They cook a lot of things quicker. So hundreds of millions of them have been sold to save people time.

Thirty years later came the next generation of ovens that manufacturers hoped would revolutionize cooking. They are called "speed cookers," because "revolutionizing" cooking still means cooking faster.

The difference, they say, is that speed cookers don't just cook faster. They cook faster with the same kind of quality appearance and taste as old-fashioned convection ovens.

General Electric introduced Advantium for $1,300. Thermador introduced at $5,700 JetDirect. Maytag introduced TurboChef for $3,000. Amana already had its speed cooker, the Wave, on the market.

With the exception of Amana, these ovens combine microwave technology (for thorough cooking) with other technology for appearance, bite and taste.

So 30 years after microwaves, manufacturers continue to invest hundreds of millions of dollars to try to cut a few minutes off the baking time of lasagna and the broiling time of a T-Bone without losing eye and taste appeal.

Thus, the primary definition of customer service in the home-cooking appliance industry remains saving the buyer's time without sacrificing quality.

From $1,300 to $5,700 seems very dear for a small oven that will save the owner 10 or 15 minutes a few times a week. But, then, five or six hundred bucks for a microwave to salvage a stale 35¢ donut seemed pricy, too.

As all people, nations, tribes become civilized, they increase their wealth and possessions and decrease their inventory of time. At some point, each individual crosses a line at which time is more valuable than money.

Saving consumers time grows every day as the leading definition of innovation or customer service or reason to buy in almost every product and service category.

If you're not working to save your customers time, you're probably working on the wrong thing.

52 | People don't eat twice that which tasted bad the first time.

We are closing in on a population figure of 300 million. There is a segment of the market for almost anything, but what determines the size of each segment?

In consumable goods markets, two important factors are consumer habits and *preventive* products.

Products that take advantage of existing consumer habits are more successful than those that do not. The road to corporate deprivation is paved with efforts to convince consumers to change their habits.

Preventive products often get a lot of publicity but seldom capture a sizable market share long-term.

The food market is a tasty or yucky example.

For 10 or 15 years, the watchwords of food marketing were lite, no-salt, low fat, low calorie, low carbohydrates. The hottest new line in supermarkets was Healthy Choice, the flagship of good-for-you groceries. The market boomed in, virtually, every food category and then receded in most.

Healthy eating is preventive.

Preventive of everything from heart disease to cancer. There will always be a market in some categories for foods that don't contain bad-for-you stuff. In many others, though, the preventive will become even less important than before, while the cures, crash dieting and doctoring continue to grow.

What makes the fate of the preventive predictable are consumer habits. The dominant habit is to eat for pleasure, not to stay alive. We eat that which tastes good. We do not put into our mouths a second time that which tasted yucky the first time.

Frito-Lay says sales of light Cheetos and Doritos are "marginal to disappointing." The hottest selling new ice cream flavors are Peanut Butter Burst and Cookie Dough Dynamo. Campbell's best selling new soup flavor in 35 years is *Cream* of Broccoli.

Snack food is not really food business. It is entertainment business. People eat snack foods for fun. Observe how much longer the popcorn line is than the movie ticket line.

Yankelovich, a major research company, reported at the peak of good-for-you-food publicity that the percentage of Americans who "frequently eat" salty snacks rose from 40% to 45%.

The buzzwords for marketers are no longer "lite, less" and "low." They are "real, rich" and "full-flavor." The number of new product introductions claiming low or no cholesterol has declined steadily since 1991.

We eat what we like, and if bad things happen, we look for cures. Krispy Kreme Donut stores are opening faster than almost any other retail food brand.

Good taste arrives at the food marketing war with the big battalion. Don't get caught trying to change habits with a *preventive* product.

53 | Innovations come from individuals, not committees.

For hundreds of years man (and woman, of course) has been confounded in his efforts to melt a cold, flat, square pat of butter on a hot, round, skinny ear of corn.

Confounded, that is, until 1994. That's when the first spray butter; well, butter-flavored spray; well, I Can't Believe It's Not Butter Spray showed up in supermarkets.

Why, you ask, after decades of WD-40 spray oil and PAM spray cooking oil, did it take so long for somebody to figure out you could spray some butter-tasting stuff on your corn and asparagus? And who is this "Vegetable Hall of Fame" genius who finally made this breakthrough, anyway?

The answers to these important questions are not easy. But some light is shed by the I Can't Believe It's Not Butter brand manager, Scott Russell.

"I'm not sure why it took so long. Somebody may have tried it earlier, but we were the first ones who were able to bring it to market," says Russell.

Who did this wonderful thing, Mr. Russell?

"Well, that's not easy to say. I can't remember exactly whose idea it was. The committee's, I guess."

And how big was this committee, Mr. Russell?

"Oh, about 20 people."

The only thing 20 people ever created was a two-humps camel. Ideas of this quality come from an individual. One person said, "Hey, let's try to spray the stuff." It surely took several times 20 to make it do right, design the package and all the other stuff.

Ideas, though, come from individuals, not committees, and Russell "couldn't (or wouldn't) remember" which one it was.

Come clean, Mr. Russell. Being first, you guys must be making a killing on this stuff. "We don't divulge margins, of course, but I can tell you we can't make it fast enough."

This opportunity, as so many others, had been out there for decades. The basic technology was in place. Lots of companies other than Van Den Bergh Foods, part of Unilever, could have done it, but they didn't. Scott Russell and his bunch did.

In whatever product or service category you work, there are other ideas just as basic waiting for you to do something about them. They come not because consumers tell you they want them. They come from observing the problems consumers have with existing products and services in your category. Like trying to melt a cold, flat, square pat of butter on a hot, round, skinny ear of corn.

Then one person says, "Hey, let's try..."

PART SIX

MARKETING

Identify and create opportunities and apply the company's resources thereto for the maximum benefit of its owners.

54 | Marketing drives demand and demand drives growth.

It is traditional in most companies that the operating division is the lead dog on the sled, and that other divisions function in supporting roles.

Yet, in most companies it is not the operating division that is charged with growth and success. It is the marketing folks.

No CEO tells the chief operating officer, "We need same-store (or same-product) growth of 12% next year. What are your plans to achieve it?"

Or, "I want to expand into six new markets next year. What will you do to make those markets successful?"

Granted, the COO will have to deliver the goods and/or services to support such growth plans.

It is the chief marketing officer, though, who will be responsible for creating that 12% increase in demand. The CMO must devise strategies to deliver sufficient customers in those new markets.

The more successful the company, the more likely it is that marketing, not operations, is the lead dog. Why? Because marketing, not operations, drives demand, and demand drives growth.

Thus, operations should answer to marketing, because marketing does not begin where operations end. Marketing begins with operations.

Marketing begins with the critical decision of which products a manufacturer should make, which to drop, which to add.

Marketing, not manufacturing people, should determine the product-benefit and price-point objectives of manufacturing. Marketing departments should determine retailers' merchandise mix and pricing.

The CMO should determine a service company's services, and what's on the menu in restaurants.

Of all the tools available to marketing officers, nothing is more important than products, services, pricing, menus and quality.

If operating people don't answer to the CMO, she can't be held responsible for success. Her other tools, such as advertising and sales promotion, are compromised if operations are flawed.

"Chief marketing officers have ideas, and they try to sell them to the guys with line authority. Most of their work is not done against competitors; it's done internally trying to get...people to let them do things," according to Gary Loveman, Harrah's CEO. "That's a losing battle."

When Steak 'n Egg Kitchen restaurants hired its best marketing director, he visited all 430 restaurants. He found that all were dirty, and ordered 430 new brooms. The operations chief blew up, and told the CMO where he could put the brooms.

When the CEO sided with operations, the marketing guy told him, "I can't achieve your revenue objectives if I can't assure that the restaurants are clean." Then he quit.

Steak 'n Egg no longer exists.

55 | Mistaking strategies for objectives is an easy road to failure.

There are as many formats for a marketing plan as there are marketers. Common to most, though, is confusion between objectives and strategies.

An *objective* should be the ultimate, desired result. Something you want to make happen. In most companies, the primary objective almost always is to increase profit. A *strategy* is what you do to make it happen. Yet most marketing plans list strategies in the objectives column.

For example, it's not uncommon to read a plan for a retailer that lists objectives such as, "open three new stores" or "expand Store No. 8." While these may be worthwhile *strategies* to increase revenue, and, therefore, possibly increase profits, they should not be *objectives*.

Both are readily achievable strategies that may not contribute to your real ultimate objective, profit. You could build or expand, then applaud and say you achieved both marketing objectives.

The presumption is that you built or expanded to make more money. You might, indeed, have made less money. It is dangerous to call those strategies objectives because you focus all attention on building and expanding, and you lose sight of the real objective, more profitable revenue.

Marketing plans for consumer products often list objectives such as increasing consumer top-of-mind awareness by 3%, market share by 2% or opening two new sales territories. These are strategies, not objectives. You could achieve all three, but make less money if you overspend to add awareness, or cut prices too low while adding share.

Strategies are pretty easy to achieve. Buy enough advertising or cut prices low enough, in the above examples, and you can increase awareness and market share and open new territories.

CEOs who don't carefully scrutinize their marketing plans for such misnomers run the risk of aggressive marketing and sales folks who set predictably attainable strategies as false objectives. They forget the discipline of examining each strategy along the way to be certain that the strategies are, indeed, getting them to the real objective.

That real objective must be, ultimately, to increase profits by either increasing margins on existing revenue and/or increasing revenue without disproportionately decreasing margins.

Marketing plans need measurable objectives. If they can't be measured, achievement can't be verified. Plans need strategies to achieve the objectives and a list of tactics to be employed to make the strategies work. They need deadlines for each, responsibility (who gets fired if it doesn't get done) and a budget for each.

Good marketing plans begin, though, with a clear understanding of the difference between an objective and a strategy.

56 | How you define your business determines its potential.

The most famous article ever written about marketing was authored by Theodore Levitt for the *Harvard Business Review* in 1960. It is titled "Marketing Myopia" and affectionately referred to by marketing students as, "Me Railroader."

Many of Levitt's examples are dated. His principles remain alive and well.

Levitt's premise is that railroading started down the toilet because management defined its business as railroading rather than transportation. When the opportunities arose to develop long distance trucking and airlines, it was the railroads, according to Levitt, that should have developed them.

There are plenty of more recent examples of Levitt's principles. Take Sears.

Levitt would say that Sears management believed it was in the department store business, rather than retailing. How else do you explain the fact that Kmart and Wal-Mart, not Sears, created discount mass merchandising on a national scale?

How else do you explain the daddy of mail-order catalogs floundering in a boom era of mail-order catalog selling? Why didn't Sears develop the Wal-Mart concept? Why didn't Sears develop specialty catalogs?

What industry should have conceived overnight delivery? Airlines, with thousands of planes, pilots, hangars, maintenance people, freight agents or the kid at Yale who dreamed up FedEx?

The railroads, Sears, the airlines missed those opportunities, Levitt would say, not because somebody else filled those needs, but because they were not filled by the obvious companies.

Market leaders create new competition when they quit innovating and start protecting. We read of bankruptcy by Schwinn Bicycles for much the same reason. Schwinn fought to protect against the innovators, rather than being an innovator.

Schwinn allowed competitors to develop the mountain bike. So America's last major manufacturer took bankruptcy when the bicycle industry was booming.

Transportation, retailing, mail order, cycling are all still growth industries. Railroads, department stores, general merchandise catalogs, traditional bicycles are not.

Many of us become experts in our industry segments but overlook the industry. Many of us focus on the entire industry and overlook segmentation opportunities.

Segmentation requires that you narrow the definition of your business. Yet, if you lose sight of the big picture, you run the risk of defining your business so narrowly that you overlook potential innovations.

Even yesterday's buggy whip maker might be alive if he'd defined his business as stimulating an energy source, rather than buggy whips. He might be selling fan belts to AutoZone.

What is the definition of your business? What could it be? What should it be? Somebody's in her den or his garage right now working on an innovation to make you obsolete. Are you?

57 | Never confuse luxury with quality.

One of the unsettling things happening in manufacturing is the synonymous treatment of quality and luxury. They simply aren't the same. One is not a substitute for the other.

When car buyers first cried, "Get out the bugs," U.S. automakers answered not with better quality, but luxuries. More stuff. More gimmicks. It's comforting to learn that German competitors, too, have succumbed.

You bought a Mercedes, thinking to yourself, finally, here is the ultimate quality machine. Wrong. Copious gimmickry and luxury, but the quality is about 75% of your daughter's Honda.

The answer, clearly, is a BMW. Of course, you get the most expensive model they make. Now you have the ultimate in a high-quality driving machine. Wrong. At 50,000 miles the mechanic says, "She'll be just like new for about $14,000."

About $100,000 later you have learned. Luxury and quality are not synonymous. Germans made them all, but there was no similarity in quality between your three Volkswagen Beetles and your two Mercedes and BMW.

The VWs? Now, there was quality. They didn't provide the outside temperature, had no onboard computers, but they ran forever without repairs.

Luxury stands for convenience, material abundance. Quality, on the other hand, means consistent performance. Many items of average quality cost a bundle because they contain material abundance.

In your kitchen drawer, there's a 30-year-old wooden spoon for which your mom spent about 29 cents. Now there's quality. You've bought several electric mixers, one of which may still work. The wooden spoon, of course, still works.

If you opt for the added convenience/luxury of an electric carving knife it's not low quality if it doesn't last forever. It is if the blades don't fit properly. If you want your car to include a gizmo to show you if the road is likely to be freezing, that's luxury. That does not make it a quality automobile or keep the doors from popping when opened.

The principle isn't restricted to manufacturing. Your cleaner *delivers* your cleaning. That's a luxury. He puts 'em in *plastic bags*. That's a luxury. Your pants-leg has one too many creases. You have a lousy quality cleaner with luxury features.

It's easy for any business to lose its quality focus and start concentrating on luxury features. Yet you eat most often where the food, not the decor, has good taste.

It's progress when Billy adds a cherry at his lemonade stand, but if he waters down the lemonade to pay for the cherry, he has lousy quality lemonade.

Get the quality right. Then add the luxuries.

58 | Any strategy might work if the strategists worked.

Nearly two-thirds of 778 major corporations polled by Louis Harris & Associates said they would change marketing strategies within the next five years.

No wonder we have worldwide recessions.

The survey found that 75% of the companies had already started revising their business processes. More than half had created strategic alliances. Most had "fierce commitments to remake (their) competitiveness."

Finally, these companies, all of which exceed $250 million annual sales, said that staying cost-competitive would be more important strategically than any other external factor.

Alliances are as old as the Bible. Staying competitive is basic for survival, and most annual reports claim that the company intends to be the low-cost producer in its industry.

But two-thirds of these quarter-billion-dollar-plus companies plan to change marketing strategies? What a waste.

Frito-Lay, dominant player in the tough snack food category, increases sales and profits every year. It may not be written anywhere, but a Frito-Lay marketing strategy is *to make it easier to buy Frito-Lay snacks than any other.*

Marketing strategies don't get any simpler. The tactic is

distribution, and at Frito-Lay distribution is an art.

Frito-Lay is dedicated to getting a snack truck, lorry, rickshaw or llama-back at the door of every potential seller of snacks in the world more often, with more snacks than anyone else.

Certainly, that has required changing business processes, multiple alliances and scrupulous attention to cost-competitiveness. Surely, it has meant changing tactics from time to time or market to market. But change marketing strategies? Not on your Frito Bandito.

The poll suggests that this strategy juggling is coming as a result of global competitiveness. That suggests that many strategists believe that their current strategies won't stand up domestically against foreign competition and/or that current strategies are not exportable.

Yet chances are that if current strategies were adequate to create $250+ million annual sales, they aren't ready to be trashed.

Management often mistakes weaknesses in execution for strategic weakness. It's more likely that currently successful strategies will continue to work if the strategists work harder executing.

Tactics may change, but sound strategies are based on human nature and market positioning. Worldwide, people buy more of brands that make it easier to buy. That's the basic principle on which Frito-Lay strategy is founded.

The principle won't change. Why change the strategy?

Other equally basic principles spawn strategy development, such as low-price leadership (Wal-Mart), innovation (Microsoft) and quality (Honda). It's unlikely that Frito-Lay or these three are planning strategy changes.

Strategy is child's play. Tactical execution is hand-to-hand combat.

59 | Before you squeeze into a niche, be sure it will support you.

Segmenting a smaller, specialized segment of a large market has been a successful marketing strategy for centuries.

It's easy today to expand a new, niche product fast due to the growth of mega-retail chains. Franchising makes it easy to expand new service and retail concepts quickly. Of course, if you make a mistake, misjudge the segment, the consequences are also greater.

If you decide to carve out a piece of a large market, you'd better know that the size of the piece you're going after is big enough and has growth potential. You'd better know, too, that your product or service isn't just a fad, and that its appeal is more than local or regional.

The guy who put oil in an aerosol can found a profitable segment of the liquid oil business for WD-40. On the other hand, some very smart hombres thought there was a market segment for liquid toothpaste.

The good colonel from Kentucky thought he could strike it rich selling only chicken, and he did. Then bagels? Get serious.

Fried chicken was a staple nationally. Colonel Sanders just isolated it. Some kids grew up with bagels, and developed the molars to fight 'em back. Bagels got campy, and people who didn't like the tough, tan truck tires ate 'em anyway.

Within a few years, most bagel store chains were either bankrupt or for sale. Bagels weren't new in many areas, by any means, but nationally, the dogs just wouldn't eat enough of them. The demand for bagels is limited, but the supply of bagels became unlimited.

In yesterday's damn-the-money-full-speed-ahead economy, everyone wanted to be first. There were a half-dozen sprinters trying to be the first national bagel chain. There were no winners.

A national chain of barbecue stores is possible, but with limited distribution. And don't confuse Starbucks Coffee, for instance, with these other niches. Starbucks created a brand with better quality in a huge, existing category. It was not a new segment any more than was chicken.

To be a successful niche player, first you must know today's size of your niche, the previous trend and forecast.

If there is no product or service on the market such as yours, learn what products/services are filling those consumer needs today and to what extent. Learn also if those needs are increasing and how much.

In most segmented marketing cases, the niche marketer's product or service is already available in some other form.

There is one thing better in marketing than being first, knowledge of the market.

| 60 | # If you want to sell underwear to women, don't design boxer shorts. |

It's always been a mystery why so many products are conceived with no consideration for a large market segment and then are promoted to attract that segment.

So when an industry that's been legendary for its product-development myopia finally gets smart, it's a marketing milestone.

Since the game was conceived, golf course developers have allowed course designers to overlook women. Courses were designed for men. Then designers threw women a bone by walking 20 yards in front of the men's tees and dropping tee markers for women.

The result is courses that are ridiculously long for the vast majority of women players.

The venerable Rocky Mountains resort, The Broadmoor, has two golf courses. On one, the 18-hole distance from the shortest set of tees is 5,573 yards with par-4 holes of up to 388 yards. On the other course, the shortest 18-hole distance is 5,921 yards with par-4s of up to 451 yards.

Very few women amateur players can drive the ball over 175 yards or hit a 3-wood over 150 yards. That means that any par-4 hole of more than 335 yards is not reachable with their two longest shots by most women. Yet 335-yard-or-less par-4s from the shortest tees are the exception on most American courses.

Now that supply exceeds demand, golf course developers finally get it. After adding everything from massages to so-called caddie-concierges for men, they are finally considering women in course design.

Bear's Best in Las Vegas offers tees with an 18-hole distance of 5,043 yards At the Thunderbirds Golf Club in Phoenix women can play tees of 4,727 yards.

On these courses, women have a chance to use more than three or four clubs in their bags. They can enjoy a round of golf that is challenging but not impossible.

About three million people take up golf each year, and about the same number quit, according to the National Golf Foundation. In 2001, the number of rounds played in America decreased.

Yet in the previous two years, 1,400 new courses were developed, or almost two per day.

Many experts agree that women are golf's greatest market potential.

You can't sell boxer shorts to women. Why should they be expected to pay to play a golf course designed for men? The best marketing investment for older courses would be a set of new, shorter tees for women.

Marketing for every product begins in the design phase. If you want the product to appeal to any market segment, that segment must be accommodated during design.

61 | Find the hottest button and push with all your might.

Every business category includes a variety of factors that determines a company's success. Call them buttons to push. There's a research button, purchasing button, packaging, distribution, sales, advertising and a host of other buttons to push that can make the business go faster.

How you apply a company's resources against these buttons has a big impact on its success. Only huge companies have the resources to apply enough pressure against every one of these buttons to make an impact. Yet most men and women in small businesses try also to apply resources against *all* the buttons.

Instead, they should identify the hottest button, that one pressure point that's more important than any other, and apply the greatest pressure there.

Consider Frito-Lay. Indeed, Frito-Lay has the muscle to push every button in the snack food marketing chain. Most responsible for its success, though, is the weight Frito-Lay has applied for decades to the distribution button. Frito-Lay pushes hard against all the marketing buttons. Foremost, though, they sell more snack food, earn more profit, because they shove the distribution button through the wall.

Frito-Lay believes, obviously, that distribution is the *most* important factor in snack food success.

On a smaller scale, most residential real estate salespeople say that the major key to success is obtaining listings. It's great to have buyers call. It's great to know all about the neighborhoods, schools and all that jazz. It's great to be a whiz-bang salesperson. But if they're covered up with enough listings of property for sale, success is guaranteed.

So the smartest residential real estate agents concentrate their efforts pushing the listings button.

To determine the strategy our company would take in pursuit of a new, multi-million-dollar piece of business, our best people were assessing our strengths and weaknesses. One bright guy said, "Our greatest strength is that we know the *right* questions to ask, and we know *whom* to ask."

Many years' experience in the prospective client's industry had taught us which was the hottest button in the category's marketing chain. That meant we knew the buttons on which to avoid wasting time and money. We knew which questions to ask and whom to ask. That put us in a position to be of help to the client faster than our competitors.

Experience and asking the right people the right questions almost always teaches you what is the primary problem to be overcome. It's easier then to figure out which button will have the most impact on the problem. With all the resources you possess, push there.

62 | Most customers don't understand your business.

It is devilishly hard to sell something if people don't know you have it for sale or don't know they need it.

One of the advantages of manufacturing and retailing is that customers can see and touch the goods. If you are in the service business, that's not the case, and you're at a serious disadvantage.

Potential customers can't see bank services, can't touch and feel insurance protection, an auto tune-up, moving or almost any other kind of service. To sell any service you have to *tell* people what you do and make it relevant. It's remarkably common for service businesses to fail to tell people everything they offer.

So it's not unusual to hear customers say, "Gee, I didn't know you could do that, too."

Almost every service provider assumes that outsiders know much more about his business than they do. The fact is, most people who aren't in insurance, for instance, know almost nothing about insurance and care even less.

So-called sales calls by bank personnel are a good example. These great-looking, well-groomed, well-educated, articulate young folks with bright faces sit down in your office. They reel off a litany of services and assume that you know what each is all about. The conversation ends, invariably, with, "Let us know if there's anything we can do for you."

You aren't a banker. You don't know whether you need the service or not. You still don't know what they can do for you.

Service providers must be able to relate what they do to the customer's business. The unbeatable solution is to know a lot about the customer. If you really know your customer's business, you can apply your services and make them relevant and desirable.

If all you know is your own business, you can speak only your language, and that may be Greek to the listener.

The most effective sellers of service are people who know how to ask questions and know the right questions to ask. You will never meet a customer who does not like to talk about his business. Give him a chance.

A little knowledge is dangerous for a buyer. A guy whose car is running rough might tell a mechanic he wants new spark plugs. The problem might be the oxygen sensor. An insurance buyer may ask for prices on the wrong coverage.

If you don't ask the right questions, buyers apply their own limited knowledge of your business, make their own decision and select, generally, only on price.

Ask, and ye shall receive.

63 | Price policy drives consumption. Consumption drives repurchase.

When they think about it, most business people realize that consumption is the key to repurchase. Few of them, however, take consumption into account when setting prices and payment policies.

Yet it's a fact that the manner in which price and payment are established influences not only original demand but also how buyers use a product or service.

Research by a couple of professors that was reported in the *Harvard Business Review* offers insight into the effect of pricing policies on consumption.

Their research shows that the more that people are aware of the cost of what they buy, the more likely they are to use it. The sooner after payment that they use it, the more aware they are of the cost.

Sound like double-talk?

Health club members who pay for memberships quarterly use their memberships more often, and are more likely to renew their memberships, than those who pay annually. Those who pay monthly use and renew their memberships more than those who pay quarterly.

A consistent pattern showed up in areas such as theatre and magazine subscriptions and sports season tickets. Timing of payment dictates level of consumption. Consumption dictates repurchase.

For a summer festival that included four plays, the professors discovered that the no-show rate for advance purchasers of all four plays was 21.5%. No-shows for three-play buyers was 13.1%, 3.5% for two-play buyers and only 0.6% for one-play buyers.

Obviously, the less that people use what they buy, the less likely they are to repurchase.

The professors learned also that cash payment results in greater consumption than credit card payment. They noted a no-show rate for credit card customers of one theatre company that was 10 times greater than for cash customers.

"People are better able to remember the cost of products if they pay with cash than if they pay with credit cards."

Clearly, the more people use a product, the more they're likely also to recommend it to friends.

Americans who carry plastic, according to *The Wall Street Journal*, "have an average of nearly eight cards in their wallets." The less they use a card, the less likely they are to renew it.

That's why credit card companies have introduced mini-cards that don't go into a billfold. They go on a key ring. A mini-card is more accessible and doesn't have to compete with other cards when a user opens his wallet.

The key to long-term customer relationships is consumption. One important factor of consumption is pricing and payment policy.

64 | It's great to be Cadillac until there's Mercedes.

It always has been a popular strategy to stake out a marketing position based on being the highest or lowest price in a business category. Popular but risky.

In every category there is a market at the top of the price scale (highest price suggests highest quality) and another at the very bottom. The majority of brands slug it out in between as middlemen in a high-low poker game.

The pitfall that awaits brands that have been positioned at either the top or bottom price level is that price is quantitative. When new brands enter the market higher than yesterday's highest or lower than the lowest, the new brands seize those positions.

For decades Cadillac defined the high-price automobile position in America. German and Japanese imports redefined the position and shoved Cadillac back into the pack. As a middleman, Cadillac struggled for decades.

Wal-Mart decimated most discount stores.

"In supermarkets, low price is no longer an ownable position," according to Laura Ries, whose daddy, Al Ries, is one of the co-coiners of "brand positioning."

Smart supermarket brand managers have abandoned efforts to position their brands as low-price leaders. Farmer Jack, a Detroit chain, ditched "It's always savings time at Farmer Jack." Now, "It's down-to-earth goodness at Farmer Jack."

If people are interested only in the lowest price, they join Sam's Club and drive home a tank truck of ketchup.

This trap of staking out the highest or lowest price positioning, only to lose it to a newcomer, is not a sudden phenomenon. It's been going on since farmers bartered fresh corn for a sack of sugar. Recent examples such as Cadillac, Absolut Vodka, Rolex Watches, discount stores and supermarkets simply focus attention thereon.

Absolut owned the premium vodka position in the U.S. for two decades. Then it started leaking market share to higher-priced, super-premium vodkas.

Absolut enjoyed a 20-year rise from 0.01% share of a 740,000-case market to 12.2% share of a 39-million-case market. New, $25 super-premium brands picked off 1.5% and 0.8% shares, while $18 Absolut lost 0.5%. Experts believe Absolut's decline will continue.

It's wonderful to be "the Cadillac" of automobiles until there's a BMW, Lexus and Mercedes. Positioning any brand on its price is tenuous at best.

Better positioning for the long haul may be Saturn's, for value, or Volvo's, for safety. These positions are more defensible, because they are qualitative, not quantitative.

Price positioning is the most quantitative. You're the highest or the lowest, or you're not.

65 | When Cokes went up a nickel, whisky sales dropped 50%.

Memo from George Pamphyllis, Sales Manager, Calvert Distillers, to Hal McGregor, sales rep, Albany, GA, Dec. 31, 1972: *"Congratulations on averaging 700 cases per month of Calvert Whisky half-pints. Keep up the good work."*

Memo from Pamphyllis to McGregor, June 30, 1973: *"Please advise reason for drop in Calvert Whisky half-pint sales from 700 cases per month to 300 cases."*

Memo from McGregor to Mr. Pamphyllis, July 2, 1973: *"Regarding your inquiry about decrease of Calvert half-pint sales, the price of Coca Cola went up a nickel."*

Memo from Pamphyllis to McGregor, July 5, 1973: *"What in the hell does the price of Coke have to do with a 400-case decrease in Calvert half-pints?"*

Memo from McGregor to Mr. Pamphyllis, July 7, 1973: *"In Albany, all I have is $2 buyers. They used to buy a Calvert half-pint for $1.85 and a 15¢ Coke. When Coke went to 20¢, they started buying $1.80 whisky."*

No product exists in a vacuum. In selling, many factors are relevant.

Marketers understand that factors such as new products and price changes by competitors can have a major impact on their own sales. They understand the impact of weather and seasonal factors.

Many marketers overlook, though, the impact that seemingly unrelated factors have on their businesses.

They should be aware constantly of factors outside their own categories that can affect performance. First, they must know what customers are buying, not what marketers think they're selling.

The Calvert sales manager thought folks were buying half-pints of whisky. Actually, they were buying whiskey and Coke, and they had only $2

If you're selling $2 Pronto Pups at the county fair, you're not in the food business. You're in entertainment. If a kid thinks another ride will be more fun than eating a Pronto Pup, the ride's where his two bucks are going.

If you're selling football tickets, you're not in the football business. You're in entertainment. Your primary competition is not, necessarily, another football game. It's all the other entertainment options.

If there's one factor in the marketing chain about which most companies have the least knowledge, it's a clear understanding of why consumers buy what they buy and how they use it.

When you know that, you'll be able to define your category accurately. You'll be in a position to read outside factors that might affect your category as well as category factors and trends.

If you know your customers are buying whisky and Coke, you won't have to ask why a price increase in Coke hurts your sales.

66 | One strong benefit beats a passel of pygmies.

Is it best for a brand to be known for one benefit or several benefits? You'd think the more the merrier. Two or three consumer benefits must be better than only one. Usually not.

A group of us from around the country was debating the issue recently.

Start with the reality that if you're very skillful and somewhat lucky, you may be able to impress on consumer minds one thing about a brand. If you beseech consumers to remember several things, well, no marketer is that skillful or that lucky.

That said, what about Colgate Total Toothpaste? Total has just about every benefit known to toothpaste. Indeed, but Colgate turned them all into one benefit. *Total has everything.*

This single, memorable benefit of Total's multiple benefits was possible because toothpaste makers previously had segmented the market by individual benefit and created high awareness for each. Fluoride brands fight cavities. Others fight tartar build-up. Others whiten. Still others sweeten your breath.

Colgate put all those top-of-mind benefits into one product, called it Total, and they won big.

It wasn't necessary for Colgate to explain or extol each individual benefit of Total. Other brands already had educated consumers.

Consumers got the point immediately, because the Total brand name says it simply and brilliantly.

One strong benefit message is critical for packaged goods if manufacturers expect consumers to remember a reason to buy the brand.

What about other products, high-ticket items, for example, in which a retail salesman is involved? You can train a retail salesman to remember a bunch of benefits if your product is the only brand he sells, such as a Buick salesman.

If she's selling in a retail furniture, clothing or department store, however, she may have to sell dozens of products of several different brands. It's nigh impossible to train such a sales person to remember several features about several brands.

Almost every retail salesman will sell most often the product in the store that is the easiest to sell. Invariably, that's the one about which she or he knows something. Product knowledge is a retail salesperson's Teddy bear.

No manufacturer has the capacity to teach its retailers several things about its brand if those retailers sell competitive brands that are trying to do the same thing.

Thus, the winning packaged goods brand generally is the one that implants one powerful reason to buy in consumer minds. The high-ticket winner is the brand that fixes one powerful reason to sell in retail salesmen's minds.

67 | Choice is good.
Too many choices is bad.

Buying telephone service in America used to be easy. You called AT&T. Today there are so many choices that buying service is maddening.

Choice is good. Up to a point.

Two social psychologists wrote a paper in which they stated that, while they like options, increasing the number of options you give people reaches a point at which it becomes counterproductive.

The New York Times reported that Columbia University's Dr. Sheena S. Iyengar and Stanford's Dr. Mark R. Lepper found that providing too many options, especially when the differences are small, can overwhelm people. Customers become less likely to buy any of the options.

They cited two experiments to prove the point. In a Menlo Park, CA supermarket, two jam-tasting displays were set up. One had six jams to taste. The other had 24 different jams.

Of 242 shoppers, 145 stopped to taste at the display of 24 jams. Only 97 stopped to taste at the six-jam display. Yet only seven of the 145 tasters at the 24-jam display actually bought a jar of jam, while 72 of the 97 tasters bought jam at the six-jam display.

Obviously, 24 jams are an overload.

In another test, one group was asked to buy chocolate from a selection of six Godiva flavors. Another group was asked to select from 30 different flavors. Afterwards, those who bought from the selection of 30 said that their chocolate was less tasty, less enjoyable and less satisfying than did those who chose from six flavors.

Thus, too many choices decrease sales. Option overload reduces buyer satisfaction, frustrates buyers and they regret their purchases.

Another psychologist, Dr. Barry Schwartz of Swarthmore, said that when options multiply, two things happen. Buyer expectations go up. Then the letdown is greater. Because with 100 options, "you have no one to blame but yourself if you choose poorly."

The proliferation of choices in which the differences between each is barely noticeable is largely a result of line extensions. For decades, packaged-food and health-and-beauty-aid marketers have added so many options that consumers are bewildered.

The *Times* story pointed out that when Procter & Gamble reduced its Head and Shoulders Shampoo brand from 26 to 15 choices, Head and Shoulders market share increased.

"Your choice" merchandising is tremendously appealing but only if options offer clear differences and the number of options is not overwhelming.

Most customers know what they're looking for. They want enough choice to find it, but too much choice makes it too hard to find.

68 | One shot to the heart can do more than two to the head.

The nice thing about familiarity is how much less complicated it makes both our personal and commercial lives.

It's more relaxing to be with friends than with strangers, and it's a lot easier to do business in the same stores, with the same dry cleaner, plumber and lawn service. One study reports that 80% of us would rather never have to change vendors for anything.

Maybe that's why so many companies seem to spend all their resources wooing new customers while flaunting a take-it-or-leave-it attitude with existing customers.

Either they take them for granted or they misunderstand their customers' full expectations.

A lawn care service may believe that its service amounts only to applying weed killer and grass fertilizer. A cleaner may believe that if he picks up your dirty clothes, delivers them clean and even sews on a missing button, that's all there is to cleaning service.

There's substantial evidence that consumers want more.

Simply executing the process or delivering the merchandise has never been an adequate definition of service. If companies, products and services don't connect emotionally with their customers, they will experience higher customer turnover rates than if they do.

One of America's great marketing companies, Hallmark Cards,

is proving the point and helping companies reach their customers emotionally. Hallmark's not proposing anything very high tech, mind you, just a little TLC.

One example is a telecommunications company for which Hallmark handled a customer retention program.

Hallmark sent an anniversary greeting card to customers before the anniversary of their one-year service contracts. Tucked in the card was a phone card for free minutes. The card didn't ask the customer to do anything. It was merely a "thank you."

Soon thereafter, the company sent contract renewal letters to the same customers, and the result was a rate of renewal 33% above normal.

A credit card issuer used much the same strategy to delinquent accounts. Instead of a formal dunning notice, a benign, hand-signed greeting card went in a hand-addressed envelope asking the debtor if he needed help working out his account. An 800 number was included.

The result, according to the company, was "a windfall of payments."

Service extends from the sale through payment, and it includes connecting emotionally with your customer throughout the process. You can't do that with stiff form letters and recorded telephone menus.

People find reasons to do business with companies they like and to find fault with those they don't. To reduce customer turnover, figure out how to reach each one individually and emotionally.

69 | Pinch off the suckers early, or you'll get smaller tomatoes.

It's not always the competition with which you go toe-to-toe every day that is the most troublesome. Often, it's new competition attacking from the flank and rear that you don't see coming.

New entries change the face of business categories and create new category segments that confound brand managers.

Life was simple when Coke had to deal only with Pepsi, when German brewers fought only each other and Ford was General Motors' only real challenger.

That was a time when soda pop owned the non-alcoholic U.S. beverage category, when beer dominated every liquid in Germany and when Americans chose among only GM, Ford and Chrysler products.

Those yesterdays are gone forever, and today isn't long for this world.

For all three of these examples, today's problems are compounded by new competition that changed their categories. Coke maintains its share of soda pop, but the entire soda pop segment is losing share to bottled water, sports drinks and so-called new-age beverages.

Germans still drink a can of beer a day per capita, but that's down from a pint a day 25 years ago. German brewers now must contend with Coke and Pepsi plus the same new products Coke and Pepsi are battling.

It wasn't Ford that savaged GM's market share. Imports changed the face of the U.S. automotive market.

If Coke had watched its flanks, Gatorade and Snapple might have come from the Coca-Cola laboratory. German brewers might have made distribution deals with newcomer beverages. GM could have made better, smaller cars 40 or 50 years ago.

Executives can become so engrossed in today's brand-to-brand battles that they don't realize some newcomer is pushing both ships onto a reef. They fail to see what new is happening in their categories, and that consumer tastes and perceptions of what's hip are changing.

Due to acquisitions, Coke and Pepsi now battle on many beverage fronts beside soda pop. SUVs and trucks have kept GM and Ford automotive divisions in business.

Nevertheless, next to arrogance, myopia is the most dangerous affliction for category leaders. They focus on the competition under their noses and underestimate the size of future tremors from invaders that change their categories.

To assure growth tomorrow, you have to be able to draw a picture of how your category might look tomorrow. Who and what could be there tomorrow that aren't there today?

It's like growing tomatoes. If you don't pinch off the new suckers when they appear on the plant, you'll end up with smaller tomatoes.

70 | Raising prices is a lot like cooking a frog.

The only thing business owners hate to do worse than fire somebody is raise prices. They'll try anything to avoid it.

When raw material costs go up, they find cheaper ones. When insurance goes up, they increase the deductible. When labor goes up, they try to increase productivity, use contract or temporary workers for whom they don't have to provide benefits.

Advertising and sales promotion, two business-building tactics necessary to sustain most companies, always feel the ax.

Before raising prices, most will even cut staff and decrease customer service. There is no limit to which business owners will not go to keep from raising prices. In most cases, it's the worst strategy possible.

If a great $15 filet mignon is the reason people come to your restaurant, and your cost of buying quality beef goes up, cutting the quality of the steaks you buy is a death wish. You'll fare better with a great $16 or $17 filet than with a mediocre one at $15.

In the 1990s, every U.S. ice cream maker faced drastic increases in the cost of butter fat, a primary ingredient in ice cream. No premium ice cream maker decreased the amount of butter fat in its products.

It is the very extent to which business will go to prevent price increases that creates its biggest problem. Inevitably, these efforts lead to shrinking margins. Most businesses do not enjoy such comfortable margins that they can survive lowering them for very long.

Regardless of how low inflation gets, the labor cost in every business increases annually, and labor is a primary cost factor in every company.

When companies continue cutting costs, delay raising prices and endure shrinking margins, they soon are left with no alternative. At that point prices must go up by double-digit percentages, and few businesses can survive big, one-time increases.

The logical alternative, of course, is small, digestible price increases of 2% or 3% annually or biannually. Such a strategy may cause a brief blip in customer volume, but nothing like a double-digit increase does.

In the meantime, margins are protected. With full margins a business can maintain its quality and continue its normal promotional tactics that are too costly if it's operating with lower margins.

Increasing prices is like cooking a frog. You have to place it into a pan of cool water, and slowly bring the water to a boil. If you throw the frog into boiling water, he just jumps out.

71 | There's more to *service* than performing the service.

The essence of a successful service business strategy is not so much how a company performs the actual service but how the company behaves toward its customers.

If you're in the service business, how do you define service?

The definition of laundry and dry cleaning service is not merely collecting dirty clothing, cleaning it and returning it. Does one lawn service keep lawns greener than others? One pest control company kill bugs deader than others?

Most customers can't judge the difference in the performance of one brand or another. So if a company defines the quality of its service only in terms of job performance, cleaning, greening or killing, how do customers differentiate between brands?

Customers differentiate between all of the other attributes.

Could she reach the company quickly on the telephone? Was it a good experience? Did the company make it easy to buy? Did the company come when it said it would, take the amount of time it said it would? Was the bill what the company said it would be?

In the service business, customers define service mostly by how the company behaves toward them and communicates with them.

While they may not always be able to judge the quality of job performance, all customers know when a vendor doesn't keep his

Thank you for flying Northwest Airlines. Please retain this portion of your boarding pass.

Visit us online at **nwa.com** for all your travel planning needs, from Frequent Flyer information and award travel reservations to flight status, schedules, availability and pricing.

nwa E-Ticket.

Name: LARKIN/ROBERT
Date: 27MAY04
Frequent Flyer Nbr: NW205001005
E-Ticket Nbr: NW0127503 008205
Flight: NW1684

Conf # NU8EUH
Request

Gate: A5 EXIT Seat: 15-D

Depart: St Louis 5:05PM
Arrive: Detroit 7:45PM

word about appointments, doesn't return calls promptly, stick to the quoted price, doesn't communicate often enough.

If the customer calls again, does the company recognize her and know she's a customer? Does the company call after the job and inquire about satisfaction?

The total customer experience is far more powerful than the mere benefits of the job performance. That experience is wrapped up largely in communications and dependability.

The more dependable the vendor, the higher the perception of service quality. The more the vendor communicates, the more extensive the service appears. Every opportunity to communicate with the customer is an opportunity to improve the service.

If a service vendor is to hold onto its customers and to differentiate himself to attract new customers, he must build a reputation for all those service elements for which he doesn't get paid.

One of the highest-priced floor-laying companies in town doesn't return calls promptly. One of the best quality kitchen counter outfits doesn't show up when it says it will. Regardless of the ability of their employees to lay floors and install counters, they're lousy service companies.

Customers will pay more for quality service, and they define quality as much in terms of communications and dependability as in job performance.

72 | You still can sell choo-choos if you add bells and whistles.

Of all the products, categories and brands that have disappeared in your lifetime, one that you probably wouldn't have given much of a chance to chug successfully into the new millennium is toy trains.

Today, kids are busy on the Internet, playing sophisticated computer games and riding jets to grandma's house. Most of today's youngsters, even their dads, never have ridden a train with a sleeper and dining car.

Nevertheless, Lionel recently celebrated its 100th anniversary. This raises a question. How does a company continue to succeed in yesterday's category, when others fail in growth categories?

Two other household names also celebrating notable anniversaries are 3M's 75-year-old Scotch Brand and 150-year-old Folgers Coffee. All three offer some pretty good object lessons for long-term success.

First, these companies continue to innovate and improve their products. They make their products obsolete before competition can do so.

Scotch Brand tape, for instance, has been manufactured during the past 75 years. It has been made in 900 different versions—transparent, colored, light-proof and high-temperature and innovative dispensers.

3M, a derivative of Minnesota Mining and Manufacturing Co., is even more active in renewing its sticky tape today than in the past. In 2001 and 2002, 3M expected 20% of total sales to come from new pop-up dispensers introduced in 1999.

It is in dispensing contrivances that Scotch Brand has been most active, because the easier you make it to use a product, the more it is used.

Although instant coffee had failed miserably in 1953, Folgers kept at it until, in 1958, it reintroduced instant coffee successfully.

Lionel is the most remarkable example of the three. A Lionel electric train has become a must for dads to buy their sons. So Lionel continues to improve its traditional models to appeal to dads and to the adult hobbyist and collector market segments. Digitally reproduced sounds now include voices of the crew and the train's brakes.

Each of these companies exemplifies the principle of extending the value of its brand. Their success has come, principally, not from extending value with line extensions of whiz-bang new products but by adding value to existing products.

By staying in touch with changing needs of your customers, you can reinvent your existing products with greater value. If you're selling exactly the same thing you were 10 years ago, it would be surprising if you have not lost market share.

Companies that breed successful products but then stop innovating die. Those that constantly renew their products and innovate are almost never derailed.

73 | It takes an 800-pound gorilla to grow any business category.

For a decade, the news was very bad for a fish business called tuna.

Then the No. 2 tuna brand, Bumble Bee, began an $8 million advertising campaign, its first in more than a decade. No. 1 Starkist followed with a multi-million-dollar campaign of its own, also its first in more than a decade.

Bumble Bee and Starkist created another textbook case of what happens when category leaders advertise and when they don't.

With Starkist holding 45% market share and Bumble Bee about 18%, their silence meant that the category was without leadership while neither of the two brands advertised.

The entire tuna category suffered. From 1987 to 1997, the 10 years in which the two leaders didn't advertise, tuna consumption dropped from 14 meals a year for the average American to 11. That's a 21% decrease.

Even sophisticated category leaders fail to realize the impact that their advertising has on their entire categories, as well as their own brands.

In 1998, Heinz Ketchup began advertising on television after a five-year hiatus. During the five years it was absent, Heinz share of ketchup sales slid from 50% to 47%. Just as important for a brand with half of the market, the entire category shrank.

Salsa came on like gangbusters, and some experts say salsa passed ketchup as the No. 1 sauce.

Studies during this period of ketchup decline showed that ketchup still was in the refrigerators in 97% of American households. But the job isn't to get it into refrigerators. It's to get it out of the fridge and into stomachs.

All advertising in any category benefits every brand in the category, because it increases consumer awareness of the category. The louder its voice, the greater the share of consumer income any category captures.

The more ketchup advertising, the more ketchup goes into stomachs.

Many categories suffer low consumer spending because the category voices are low. In their obsession with brand market share, many overlook category growth.

Even though a category leader may be able to cut back advertising and still hold onto his share of the market, it will lose volume if the category shrinks, and the category *will* shrink.

Americans can name more bedding brands than all other furniture store products combined. That's because three bedding makers spend more on brand advertising than all other furniture store products combined, with the exception of La-Z-Boy. So bedding commands a disproportionate share of home furnishing sales.

Brand advertising determines not only the size of the fish. It determines also the size of the pond.

74 | 100 pounds of air ruins a perfectly good 10-pound balloon.

There seems to be an assumption that any successful niche brand can be grown into a national, even international, power brand if placed in the hands of a large brand marketing company.

This assumption is the root of many unsuccessful mergers and acquisitions.

There are fundamental differences in mind-set and strategic thinking between people who create niche brands and those who have spent their careers with market leader brands.

These differences are cultural to each brand and seldom can be overcome. So the thinking of the acquirer dominates, and the strategies that made the smaller brand successful are abandoned. A profitable brand at 3% market share becomes an unprofitable brand with 5% share.

One key difference often is distribution. Niche brands often are created with limited, protected distribution.

Yardley's of London was a highly respected cosmetics line sold for many decades only in the company's elegant store in London, department stores and a few high-end drug stores. Subsequently, the company underwent several acquisitions. After each one, its distribution was expanded.

Yardley's ended up in every chain drug store and discount store.

A brand that once enjoyed an impeccable image and high margins became a low-end football kicked all over the retail map. The London store was closed, and the brand has vanished from any upper-end retailer. Yardley's is insignificant today.

Snapple was a highly successful niche brand that, after acquisition by Quaker Oats, was almost decimated.

The fundamental misunderstanding by both the Yardley's and Snapple acquirers is that in both cases the brands' limited distribution was one reason for their success.

The problem begins when the acquirer pays too much for the smaller brand. To recoup its overpayment, the acquirer must increase sales quickly. Expanding distribution is the fastest way. So there's an immediate sales spike as new pipelines are filled.

When the brand shows up everywhere, consumers perceive that the brand has lost its cache, and they lose interest. As the brand gathers dust on retail shelves, deep discounting becomes a coffin nail.

Distribution is only one factor. Other strategic differences between acquirer and acquiree include advertising and pricing policies, publicity, packaging, sales representation and every other promotional tactic.

Successful niche brands are created by entrepreneurs who operate 180 degrees from brand leaders. If Revlon or Coca-Cola geed, Yardley's and Snapple hawed. That's a basic principle of competing against a brand leader.

It is unrealistic to believe that marketers of brand leaders can change their stripes to those of a niche player. And, in most cases, they are too arrogant to allow the smaller brand's people to continue calling the shots.

75 | Dried plums outsell prunes.

By any other name a prune is still a prune, but an $89 million prune business by another name is a $100 million business.

Prune sales jumped 10 percent in 2000 when the California Prune Board decided to quit calling its brand "Sunsweet Prunes" and started calling it "Sunsweet Dried Plums."

"It was amazing," the board's vice president of global marketing, Arthur Driscoll, said. "It was the first time in five years that the category showed any growth, and we believe it came from new users," Driscoll said.

With all the prune jokes and the infamous Dick Tracy comics character, "Pruneface," it's not surprising that dried plums sell better than prunes. What's surprising is that owners of a brand with a 75% share of the prune market would take such a gamble.

In the consumer packaged goods business, any change in product identity or package design of a successful product is about as welcome as heartburn.

The slightest change on the outside of a package can bring thousands of letters accusing the maker of changing what's inside. At the very least, if consumers no longer recognize a package, they become confused and unsure that it's what they've been buying.

Yet another prominent household brand also has been taking

liberties with its package with terrific results.

Nothing in the supermarket is recognized more than Heinz Ketchup. So when Heinz plays around with the American flag of ketchup, it's serious. Surely you have seen the promotional labels the brand started putting on shelves in 2001.

Heinz Ketchup labels include one of the following seven statements: "Sunscreen for French Fries; Quiet please, tomatoes meeting inside; 14 billion French Fries can't be wrong; Not New and Improved, Not green" (on red ketchup only, of course); "Instructions: Put on food," or "Mustard looks up to it."

"We were just having some fun with the product, and people liked it. A lot of people collected the labels," Heinz spokesman, Michael Mullen, said.

Ketchup was a $300 million category in 2001. Heinz owns about 55% of the business, up from 50% before it introduced green ketchup, a whopping jump in a category that's taken it on the chin recently from salsa.

Heinz introduced purple ketchup late in 2001. Why not?

This is an object lesson for all marketers. Even household standards can be energized with new ideas. Research your ideas and be careful, but all change isn't bad. Renewing old brands can be very successful.

If dried plums sell better than prunes, imagine if catfish weren't called catfish.

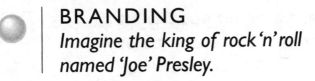

PART SEVEN

BRANDING

Imagine the king of rock 'n' roll named 'Joe' Presley.

76 | ## Make a brand positioning statement a reason to buy.

When Al Ries and Jack Trout coined "brand positioning" in 1972, they rid advertising people forever of the unflattering nickname, "sloganeers."

After Trout and Ries, slogans were no longer slogans. They became "positioning statements," a far more academic identity than slogans. Never mind that a slogan is still a slogan and that a positioning statement may, or may not, be something different. No self-respecting advertising person ever again admitted to writing a slogan.

When 7 UP called itself the "Un-Cola," that was a positioning statement. "Un-Cola" positioned in the minds of soda pop swiggers exactly what 7 UP was not, which, in the soda pop business, can be more important than establishing what you are, if you are not Coke or Pepsi.

A slogan may embody a positioning theme or it may not. For decades, the slogan, "The beer that made Milwaukee famous," served Schlitz Beer quite well. It simply was memorable word carpentry with no reference to any particular marketing position.

"Absolutely, positively overnight" was a slogan that stated brilliantly the FedEx brand position, guaranteed overnight delivery. The trouble with a mere slogan is that inadvertently it can position a brand incorrectly in consumers' minds.

A slogan for Outback Steakhouses, a source of pretty good steaks, is an example. If you had not been to Outback, but heard its slogan, you might wonder about the place.

To wit, the Outback slogan, "No rules. Just right."

"No rules" must mean something good, presumably, to the Outback people. It might be meant to imply that, as at Burger King, you can, "have it your way," not the cook's way.

You could interpret it to mean that, unlike most restaurants, there are no rules about, say, "No shirt. No shoes. No service." You might suppose also that it means there are no rules about quality purchasing, cooking, serving or cleaning up the joint.

A positioning statement is generally associated with a reason to buy. One of the oldest slogans in America is Ivory Soap's memorable "99 and 44/100th percent pure." A stronger reason to buy was Ivory's positioning statement, "It floats," when other bars of soap sank to the bottom of the tub.

In the food business, though, rules are considered by most eaters to be important. It's probably not a good idea to create either a slogan or a positioning statement around a promise that your restaurant has no rules.

Customers might believe that you'll be the next restaurant on TV news with pink slime in your ice machine and a health department warning to, "CLEAN UP."

77 | Brand awareness is grand, but awareness for what?

One adage of brand marketing is that advertising builds top-of-mind awareness, which leads to market share, which leads to profit. The brand that advertises most should have the highest top-of-mind awareness among consumers, the largest market share and profit.

Top-of-mind awareness means being the brand that consumers mention first when asked, without prompting, to name brands in a category. *Unaided* awareness goes to any brand those people can name without prompting. *Aided* awareness means those brands that consumers don't name but say, "Yes," when asked if they've heard of them.

A written objective of most brand advertising is to "increase top-of-mind awareness."

Top-of-mind awareness is a legitimate goal. In the fiercely competitive dash for awareness numbers, though, marketers have a blind spot. Many forget that consumers need the right *attitude* about a brand. Mere awareness is not enough.

Consumer attitude can be influenced by a demonstrable product difference (our ketchup is thicker). With today's product parity, though, attitude comes more often from making consumers *feel* a certain way about a brand. You're macho if you smoke Marlboro, cool if you wear Nike.

Whether the difference is demonstrable or merely perceived, it's mandatory that a brand be known for something buyers want.

Nowadays, advertising technique (and, of course, frequency) is the primary tool for creating top-of-mind awareness. Techniques such as music, celebrity personalities, special visual effects and slogans.

There was little in message to choose between Diet Pepsi's Ray Charles and Coke's soda-popping Polar Bears. Both made viewers smile. Both created high top-of-mind awareness. Consumers liked the brands, because they liked the advertising.

Attitude is absolutely critical in product categories in which a retail salesperson is involved.

As you move to bigger ticket items, you encounter the influence of retail sales people, and the benefits of top-of-mind awareness may diminish. When the influence of a retail salesperson is added, top-of-mind awareness alone may not cut it and might not be worth the cost.

You've heard, "Oh, I'll be happy to sell you Brand A, but Brand B has all the features of Brand A at a lower price. Brand B just doesn't spend as much on advertising." If you've even heard of Brand B in such cases, it stands for "BINGO."

You must be certain that your brand needs *top-of-mind* awareness. If *unaided* or even *aided* awareness will do, advertising for *top-of-mind* awareness may not be worth it.

Brand A needs a powerful consumer attitude to overcome the salesman. You should say and do the *right* things, not just anything, to build awareness.

78 | A great brand name makes everything easier and cheaper.

Haven't you wondered if you ever would have heard of Engelbert Humperdinck if he were John Smith?

Companies spend enormous sums to differentiate themselves from competition and to build name awareness. It's easier and cheaper if they start with names that are fresh and memorable.

Almost all company names fall into one of four categories. They are either proper names (Procter & Gamble), geographic (Northwest Airlines), benefit/descriptive (Budget Car Rental) or letter games, Kleenex or IBM.

The best ones tell you what the company's business is, imply a benefit, are easy to pronounce and spell. One of the great brand names is Holiday Inns. It passes all the above tests.

Now companies are as concerned about how investors, as well as customers, perceive their names. Every year, more than 100 publicly traded companies change their names.

Waste Management, Inc. changed its corporate name to WMX Technologies, Inc. The chairman said the company had never received its proper respect, because it is in the trash business.

Waste Management is not so foolish to try to fool customers. It remains Waste Management on dumpsters and in the phone book.

The less you spend to make a name well known, the more

important it is to have an almost perfect name.

If you spend enough, you can make a name even like McDonald's a household word for hamburgers. If you spend less, Burger King would serve you better.

One of the great name traps is dug with initials. GE, IBM and UPS are memorable because first each one had a sensible name. DHL has a problem.

Another name trap is the geographic category. If you pick a geographic name that describes your market today, it might not tomorrow. It was a huge blunder when Northwest Airlines merged with Republic and chose to retain the name Northwest instead of Republic.

Back Yard Burgers has spent little, comparatively, on advertising but has an easier task than competitors. The name is fresh and includes a perceived benefit.

To pour money into an obscure, confusing or meaningless name is throwing today's money after yesterday's flush. There are plenty examples of companies changing names and achieving higher awareness in 12 months than they had achieved in the prior 25 years with the old ones.

In the rush to create names that sound important, corporations choose names such as Allegis, the holding company for United Airlines, which has been described as sounding like the next world class disease.

Nothing you do is more important than creating a name for your brand.

79 | Brand icons can achieve immortality.

Charlie the Tuna is back. So is Speedy Alka-Seltzer. The puzzle is why they ever left.

The Keebler Cookie elves, Michelin Tire man, Pillsbury Doughboy and many other well-known product and brand icons haven't skipped a beat. Such personality-giving, awareness-building devices only become more valuable each time they appear.

That's why it's so puzzling when marketing people decide that icons have out-lived their usefulness. Even more so for Speedy, because Speedy, indeed, represents the all-time epitome of product icons.

Speedy is not artistically pleasing. In no way cuddly, as is the little fabric softener bear.

Yet Speedy not only represents the product. He is made from the product itself, a wafer. Since Alka-Seltzer wafers are not visible in the package, Speedy's wafer torso lets people see what's in the package before they buy. That's a benefit.

What distinguishes Speedy from other icons, though, is his name. Speed is the No. 1 product benefit, the No. 1 reason to buy. If you have a headache, indigestion or a hangover, you want speedy relief. You want Speedy Alka-Seltzer.

Charlie, the StarKist Tuna, left the advertising scene in 1988.

StarKist was the category leader then and remains so today with about 45% of the tuna market.

Charlie's hiatus from TV had little effect on StarKist's market share, but it had an impact on StarKist's overall sales. From 1987 to 1996, the tuna category decreased by more than 21%.

The dominant factor was a decrease in category advertising impact from the absence of Charlie. The brand leader in any category bears the responsibility not only for brand growth but for category growth, as well. Charlie is more than a brand icon. Charlie is the tuna category icon.

It took StarKist a long time to take full advantage of Charlie, but they appear to have learned now. Charlie appears now on the can and on point-of-sale displays.

When considering an icon for any brand, there are a few basic principles. Try to build the brand name into the icon name. In the case of Charlie, you have to remember what tuna brand he represents. Not with Speedy Alka-Seltzer.

Design the icon around the product. The Michelin man is made of tires. The Pillsbury boy is dough. Build all advertising and promotional materials around the icon. Get the icon onto the package, the store sign, the product, everywhere.

Snoopy does a great job for MetLife, but he never will represent the brand exclusively. There's no question about Speedy Alka- Seltzer.

80 | Bad package design is a salesman with gravy on his tie.

No respectable sales person would trot out on her or his rounds in a dirty, unpressed suit and beat-up shoes. Yet retail shelves still are crowded with products in label designs, sales dress, that quivocate that.

Since more than 60% of buying decisions are made after a consumer reaches the store, it is brand masochism.

Despite the billions of dollars spent to build brand awareness, there remain many product categories in all stores with little or no brand recognition among consumers. It's in these under-advertised categories that products benefit most from smart package design.

In 1992, wild birdseed was a half-billion-dollar category in the U.S. Margins are too low to support brand-building advertising budgets. So Kaytee Products of Wisconsin redesigned its plastic bags, shedding their industrial look for colorful, consumer-oriented appeal.

In the next five year's, Kaytee's sales ballooned from $10 million to $90 million. The new package design didn't just sell Kaytee faster in its traditional hardware store distribution. It allowed Kaytee to gain new distribution in pet food stores and supermarkets.

Even in highly advertised categories, product name and package design have enormous impact. An unsuccessful brand of potato chips called "Deli Chips" was renamed Dirty Potato Chips in an entirely new package design and became a multi-million-dollar brand without advertising.

Jergens Lotion, as old as the hills, fell to No. 2 in its category. After a total package redesign to look more expensive, Jergens sales shot up 30%.

When retail sales clerks disappeared, packaging became critical. Full color package design looks like higher quality to consumers. Products in boxes have better images than those in bags. A bottle inside a box has more perceived value than a naked bottle.

Almost nothing beats unique package design. Look at Ungentine's fire extinguisher, Janitor in a Drum and Mr. Clean. These products go for decades without significant advertising and retain huge sales volumes through memorable packaging.

Others opt to avoid up-front investments in great design and custom container molds. They buy stock containers and end up paying more through failure or higher marketing costs.

When somebody brings a great design or a unique name to the marketing committee, it's like a naked streaker in the room. Then, somebody says, "Oh, I understand it all right, but people won't get it. They won't understand. Besides, it's too expensive."

Every company should have a large, body-sized cannon in which to place and fire into oblivion everyone who ever says, "Oh, I get it. I like it. But *they* won't, and it's too expensive."

81 | Get the brand on the product, not just on the package.

A brand label used to be only a symbol that there was something of value about a product. Today, on many products, the label itself is the value.

In most categories, knock-offs and product parity have changed the entire concept of branding. Once out of the package, many well known products lose their identity. If those brands can't extend their identity through the life of the product, they may lose their cachet.

In the early 1950s, an American dressmaker, Vincent Draddy of David Crystal, Inc., bought the Izod name from a London clothier. Then he teamed up with French tennis star, Rene Lacoste. By the 1980s, annual sales of shirts with embroidered alligators reached $596 million.

Today, there's not a closet in any developed country without clothing articles with a brand label on the outside as well as inside. Golf pro shops couldn't exist if they sold only golf shirts without the course logo splashed on front.

Heads, chests, backs, wrists, hands, waists, fannies, ankles, feet, all have become display space. People all over the world are simply billboards with legs.

This is no mere clothing phenomenon. Macho hombres pay

big bucks for automotive tires with the brand name molded in big white letters.

Take the Nike swoosh off a pair of $150 sneakers, and you have a $50 pair of sneakers. Remove the emblem and change the grille on a $50,000 Mercedes, and you have a $30,000 car. In many categories, the brand identity, not the product performance, is the measure of value.

One reason furniture is a dog category in share of consumer spending is because furniture makers have never been able to figure out how to get a label on the outside that'll stay on in the home. A La-Z-Boy with a label on the foot-rest could overcome the gazillion Brand X recliner knock-offs.

Hunter was urged to prominently display its logo on its ceiling fans to separate them from cheap, imported look-alikes. It took almost 10 years to get it done. It's still not big enough.

You know that chocolate cookie with the white cream in the middle? The Oreo name is smack dab in the middle on both sides of each one. It's visible all the way to the shadow of your nose. Hot dog makers should figure out how to get the brand on each dog.

If you're spending money to build a brand, get it on the product itself, not just the package, and make sure it stays on 'til the last second of product life.

82 | Create a legend for your brand.

Americans like new stuff. Yet in most brands that we buy and companies with which we do business, we Americans place great value on substance, tradition and roots.

One way to make your brand or your company more interesting, more memorable, desirable and successful is to create a legend therefor.

The legends behind products such as Jack Daniels Whiskey and Gatorade have differentiated those brands from competition almost since their introductions.

Gatorade marketing has been centered on the legend of the University of Florida professors who developed the product, tested and proved its benefits with the Florida Gators football team.

Hewlett-Packard advertises regularly on network television the legend of the two young founders who developed the company's first product in a barn. The legend of Colonel Sanders and his "secret recipe of 11 herbs and spices" remains a linchpin of KFC advertising worldwide.

Jeep reminds today's buyers of why the Jeep was born and of its critical role in World War II. To advertise today's Jeep SUVs, they show black-and-white film of Jeeps bouncing across European battlefields in the 1940s.

Legends foster credibility. They intrigue consumers, because we all like good stories. People who are bored by product facts are fascinated by product stories.

In the 1930s, we read the story of the laboratory mistake that created Ivory, the first bar of soap that floated, didn't sink to the bottom of the bathtub.

All consumers are drawn to companies and brands that are run by people who demonstrate a passion for what they do. Legends document passion. Millions of Americans know the story of Fred Smith's college paper that was the seed of FedEx.

Most of the hundreds of books written about specific American corporations include fascinating stories of the founding of those companies. It's a pity that more of those companies haven't taken advantage of their warm, personal legends to balance the curse of the huge, impersonal corporation.

This is not hard to do. Who started your company and why? What were the circumstances and difficulties? What was the dream, the passion of the founder(s)?

Remember Abe Plough and his pushcart that became a giant pharmaceutical company.

A friend in Hickory, NC, operates a popular restaurant and motel called Mull's. "The Legend of J. Pearly Mull," his father-in-law, who opened a hotdog stand on the site in the 1940s, is featured on every menu.

Walk into a room and announce, "I have some important facts for you." Count how many heads turn. Then walk in and say, "Listen to this great story." Everyone pays attention.

PART EIGHT

SELLING

Whatever your job, you'll be better if once you toted a bag.

83 | Hear what the 'Snuff King' of Gilchrist County sayeth.

Chap Martin was the baby of his mama's 22 kids. Reared rock hard. Out of the sack at 4 every morning, beating the bushes of northern Florida by 6.

Chap packed 250 pounds on six-feet and an inch. Despite his pipe and uncommon intelligence, you wouldn't mistake Chap for any Ivy Leaguer. Around Gilchrist County, Chap Martin was the snuff king.

He was a salesman for American Snuff Company and a keen study of customers and nitty-gritty.

Chap wrote only one-page orders. "Don't ever let a buyer see you go to a second page. He figures he's already spent too much. Just start writing in the margins, between the lines, but don't turn the page."

At every country store, he bought a penny box of matches so the owner'd open the cash register, and Chap could peek inside. "If I see a couple tens or twenties in that till, I know just what size order to pitch him."

"No" was a word Chap held against you. If a customer uttered the ugly word, Chap couldn't forget it. He worried over it. Pondered that "No." Then he set his mind to figuring out what to do about it.

Take the day Chap went in to present the new peach-flavored

snuff to a good customer. This store sold more snuff than any other in the county, mostly Chap's snuff.

The owner had no hankering, though, for peach snuff. Didn't like the taste himself. Didn't think anybody else would. Chap spent that whole night figuring.

He pulled out his road map, put a dot where the store was, then drew a three-mile-radius circle around it. The next day he left a free carton of peach snuff at every single farmhouse within three miles of that store.

Then he did it all over again. For fear he might have missed somebody, he put a carton in every RFD post office box. Chap's home office complained. Didn't understand why it took a full carton.

"Why, these folks are real snuff users," Chap "Carton" Martin wrote back. "They'd be insulted with less than a full carton."

A couple of weeks later, he stopped by that store to get some gas. The screen door slammed. Chap could hear the owner's feet crunching across the gravel all the way to the gas pump.

"Martin," he said. "I ain't sold a lick of snuff in a month. What's it gonna take me to get you outta these woods?"

"'bout four cases of peach, I reckon."

84 | Don't waste your time with buying filters.

In most buying and selling equations, the costliest element to both buyer and seller is the filter between them.

The filter is the person to whom a salesman must make a sales presentation but who won't make the ultimate buying decision. The filter will interpret the presentation to the decision maker.

There's not a salesperson who doesn't waste time and money presenting to the wrong person. There isn't a buyer, whatever his title, who doesn't buy the wrong service or product frequently because he got filtered data.

Most filters judge what *they* think is important, what *they* think the real buyer needs to know. The filter has a totally different frame of reference from the buyer. He never possesses the same perspective or knowledge with which the buyer would react to any sales presentation.

The filter doesn't know what questions the buyer would ask, and he interprets strengths and weaknesses of a presentation in a light that is different from the buyer.

When the filter interprets presentations, he is selective. That's his job, but he has different biases and attitudes. If the buyer asks a question the filter hadn't thought of asking, the filter seldom says, "I'll go back and ask her that." The filter gives an opinion.

Had the buyer heard the original presentation from the salesperson, he might have learned something that would have caused him to change his own attitudes or opinions.

There are millions of books and pamphlets and training courses about selling. By now we have millions of pretty fair sales people out there who know something about selling. Yet many of them still don't know to whom they should sell or don't know how to get to her.

A salesperson who settles for presenting to anyone but the real decision maker is turning his livelihood over to a filter. A decision maker who relegates to a filter the screening process in any buying decision is making a mistake.

If you're trying to sell Mr. and Mrs. Jones a new car, find out quick which one is the real decision maker. If you're talking to the personnel guy about a new medical plan, but the president's gonna make the decision, you'd better be there when they get together.

If, ultimately, you're the buyer, and it's important enough for you to make that decision, it's important enough for you to get the facts from the horses' mouths, not an interpretation. If it's not important enough for you to do that, then let the filter make the decision.

85 | You won't sell much if you can't read buying signals.

"What you need to understand," Clint Thomas used to say, "is that we sell ninety percent of the people who walk through the door. People browse a department store, but when they walk into Scott Appliances they want to buy an appliance."

Everybody who walked through the Scott Appliances door might as well have been wearing a sign, "I'm here to buy." Although many buying signals aren't that simple, most are, and some salespeople just don't know how to read.

Take Dave Swearingen's phone call. "I need ten thousand printed T-shirts right away." Sound like a buying signal to you?

"I'll have the boss call you back."

By the time the boss called, Dave already had bought the T-shirts. What was it about "right away" that the first guy didn't understand?

Some salespeople even shove buying signals down your throat. While in Sears, a friend saw Florsheim Shoes. He and a saleswoman located the shoes he wanted on an in-store video screen.

She glanced at the screen for the price. "Lord have mercy," said she. "You ain't gonna pay no $265 for a pair of shoes are you?" That's a true story.

Clearly, many salespeople don't know when to shut up and take an order.

Four hours into a presentation to a $2 billion division of one of America's largest corporations, the meeting was going into extra innings.

"It's service," the prospect kept saying. "How do we know you can give us the service we need?" They'd heard of staffing plans, capabilities and promises of time and devotion. Our bag of tricks was empty.

Young Bob groped inside his coat and produced his appointment calendar. He held it high for everyone to see. With a great flourish he slid it across the conference table. It came to rest in front of the Big Cheese.

"There's my appointment calendar for the next year," Bob said. "Fill it out."

The buying signal was there. "Prove you can give us the time we need." It was time for action, no more talk. Just like that, a $20 million sale.

Learn to read buying signals or learn to eat less. The hard thing to remember about selling is that, sooner or later, you have to quit meeting, quit talking and do something to close the sale. The minute you read a buying signal, do something.

Remember the story about the guy who asked the clothing salesmen if he had the suit in blue. That was a buying signal. Turning on the blue light; that was action.

86 | Never try to sell anything in a room with corners.

One of the first great lessons of life is that when painting the floor of a room you don't start at the doorway and work inward. Whence cometh the cliché, "painting oneself into a corner."

It is also a magnificent lesson for people who sell. Never paint your prospect into a corner. Another way to say it is that when selling, remove any potential corners in the way you make your presentation. Keep the room "round."

It is easy to create corners by what you say, or fail to say first. *A corner is anything that causes you or the customer to disagree.*

For instance, in the advertising agency business, every ad you present to a client is being shown to somebody who already has her own idea. You must make certain that she has no opportunity to volunteer her idea before you have finished.

You pre-conceive every possibility you can before your presentation. Then, one by one, you present all the other possibilities and explain the weaknesses of each before you get to the right one.

"We thought about doing it this way, but then we realized that was wrong because..."

One of those possibilities will be close enough to her idea, and you will have exposed her to its weaknesses before she exposed it as her idea. If she gets the chance to tell you her idea first, you are faced with telling her why she's wrong. She's cornered, and the only way out is over you.

The principle is sound whether it's a car, washing machine, computer, insurance policy, whatever. You will increase your closing rate if you eliminate the possibility of cornering the prospect.

Nobody likes to be told he is wrong. First think of all the reasons why a person might not want to buy, all of the potential arguments. Deal positively with each before the prospect can bring it up. If you handle potential objections before they are posed by the prospect, your explanations are positive. If objections are brought up first by the prospect, your explanations appear defensive and less convincing.

Putting any prospect in a corner, having to disagree with her for any reason, turns you into an adversary. People buy from people they like, and they try very hard not to buy from people they don't like. Most people don't like adversaries.

Salespeople who learn to keep the room round will assure that neither seller nor prospect ever gets cornered. Both will avoid becoming adversaries.

87 | You can't sell a service if you don't connect with a need.

You don't have to explain what to do with a hammer or how somebody will benefit from owning one.

But, if you're in a service business, you'd be amazed at how many prospects don't understand your service and why they need it. A bright, young professional in internal corporate communications told this story.

She worked hard for months trying to convince a senior executive in a big company to retain her to improve communications inside his company.

Mind you, this woman doesn't merely edit company newsletters and slap up bulletin boards in employee break rooms. The level at which she operates is complex, and the results of her work can be critical in shaping employee attitudes, retention, teamwork and productivity.

The guy never said "Yes," and he never said, "No." It dragged on until she finally pitched in the towel.

Months later, they met on the street. They'd gotten along pretty well, so she asked him why she had failed. "You seemed so interested," she said.

"I never really understood what you were talking about," he said, "and I didn't want to appear stupid asking a lot of dumb things that I probably should have known."

It's a common story. Even after hundreds of years, a lot of bankers still can't explain to small businesses how the bank can benefit them. The hurdle for most E-commerce companies is explaining why you need them.

Most of this failure lies in the provider's inability to connect his service with the prospect's needs. Not because the provider doesn't know his business, but because he doesn't know the prospect's business.

Hammers are not esoteric. Services often are. Service benefits can't be demonstrated as easily as smacking a nail into a two-by-four.

Effective service sellers learn enough about the prospect's business to show exactly how the service benefits a specific prospect. They never leave it to the sellee to figure it out.

Twenty years ago, much of Xerox's success resulted from market-centering its sales force around specific customer categories so that each salesman became an expert in one category.

When a Xerox peddler went to sell a trucking outfit, he knew almost as much about trucking as he did about Xerox.

Many of the most successful service vendors to advertising agencies are individuals who worked for years inside agencies. It's a lot easier to sell anybody if you've been a mile in her shoes.

To connect a service to a buyer, to make the benefits of a service tangible to that individual, you still gotta know the territory.

PART NINE

ADVERTISING
The highway to sales and brand equity or the deepest sanitary waste dump.

88 | It's not a matter of good or bad. Is it the right advertising?

The commercials have become as much a part of Super Bowl and Olympics television programming as the games themselves.

News coverage of the advertising almost equals that of the events. Expert opinions abound about which commercials were good and which weren't.

Obviously, judgments of good, bad, best and worst are highly subjective. Experts disagree more often than they agree. The entire exercise is meaningless, though, because it treats the advertising as though it is entertainment. That, of course, is not its primary objective.

This is not to say that advertising should be boring or that it may not be a benefit if it's entertaining. The legendary Bill Bernbach said, "You can't bore people into buying your product."

Yet the real issue is not whether somebody says it's "good" advertising or "bad" advertising. Advertising agency trophy cases are crowded with entertaining, award-winning ads and campaigns that failed the advertiser.

The issue for the company that's paying for it is whether it is the right advertising or the wrong advertising.

Media coverage of advertising and advertising awards competitions focuses almost exclusively on execution. Art directors who judge advertising consider how it looks. Copywriter judges look for clever language.

Seldom do judges consider if the advertising delivers the right message and if it ties the brand closely enough to the ad for people who remember the ad to remember also who paid for it. That is so basic as to be insulting to mention. Yet evenings are filled with TV commercials that you remember without remembering the brands.

That happens when the brand is not as important as the concept around which the ad is created. Great advertising is that which is effective for the advertiser. Invariably, such advertising emanates from the product itself. It is not based on some borrowed contrivance with the brand pasted on the end.

Granted, in many me-too categories such as beer and soda pop, there may be no unique benefits. So the issue becomes how the advertiser makes you feel about the advertising. Yet even when the advertising is of cartoon polar bears or frogs, the bears drink Coca-Cola and the frogs croak, "Bud...weis...er."

You can't remember the bears without remembering that they drink Coke or the frogs without remembering what they croak.

When advertising revolves around a reason to buy the brand, it's the right advertising. When it doesn't, it's wrong. If the right advertising then connects emotionally and memorably with the consumer, it's great advertising.

First, get your advertising right. Then make it great.

89 | Advertising success requires the 'Chinese Water Torture.'

When advertising is a major element in a brand-building strategy, no factor is more important than continuity. Think of advertising as the "Chinese Water Torture."

Yes, brand positioning, media selection, target market reach and frequency and creative strategy all are important considerations. Continuity, though, is the foundation of effective brand building advertising.

There has been a pattern for decades among some companies, even entire categories, to spend a lot for advertising when business is good and profits are high, then stop when business slows.

The primary example always has been furniture manufacturing. Advertising only periodically is the main reason that furniture gets such a low share of consumer spending, and why only one brand, La-Z-Boy, scores any real awareness among American consumers.

The next two best known brands in furniture stores aren't furniture at all, but Serta and Sealy, both bedding brands.

During the '90s booming economy, furniture makers enjoyed the greatest success in the industry's history. True to form, manufacturers spent big for advertising.

Bassett, one of the nation's largest and oldest furniture makers, announced a 50% increase in its 2000 advertising budget. It advertised on network TV, as well as in "shelter" magazines.

In *FURNITURE/TODAY*, Bassett's head of marketing was quoted that it was Bassett's return to shelter magazines, "for the first time in many, many years."

That's the problem with Bassett and the entire industry. Furniture business was poor for a long time, so almost all makers spent nothing to build their brands. When business boomed, they came out of the woodwork to spend, spend.

You can bet that, when business softens, history will repeat itself, and furniture brand advertising will dry up again.

Of course, when many furniture brands advertise, the industry's consumer voice is louder. So it takes a lot more money for any brand to be heard. When business is slow, and other brands run for cover, a brand can dominate the industry's voice for peanuts.

Brand advertising performs best without peaks and valleys. La-Z-Boy, Serta and Sealy have advertised continuously for decades. They never stop. Budgets rise in good times and fall in bad times, but they never experience huge swings.

Whether your brand is in furniture, general insurance brokerage, hot dogs, wheel alignment or package delivery, you will build it more effectively and cost efficiently if you advertise continuously, even at lower levels, than if your advertising reflects a feast or famine mentality.

Retailer advertising must yank people in today. Brand advertising is a slow, tugging process that is wasted if only periodic.

90 | ## You can change the execution but don't change the message.

We know that Wisk prevents ring-around-the-collar, Lite Beer tastes great and is less filling and Marlboro Cigarettes are macho.

We know because these messages were drummed into us for many years. It's a shame how many other companies spend millions for advertising with little to show for it, because they constantly change their advertising messages.

A fundamental principle of effective advertising is consistency. That means advertising continuously, not sporadically. It also means consistency of message. Most large advertisers understand continuity. Few understand the importance of a consistent message.

Everyone knows that "Virginia is for lovers," that the "Skies of United" were "friendly," that Ivory Soap has the credibility of being "99 and 44/100% pure." These are no longer just advertising campaigns. They are facts.

If there's one word that epitomizes great advertising, it is not creativity. It is *discipline.* Through many agencies and company VPs of advertising, all great advertisers maintain discipline.

It's okay to change advertising execution. Just don't change the message. Marlboro has had hundreds of different billboard executions, only one message. Lite Beer made dozens of TV commercials during the period. All said, "Tastes great. Less Filling."

Advertisers have two assets, time and money. Both must be invested liberally. Continually spending millions of dollars on different messages may build brand awareness, but failure to invest enough time in a single message builds awareness without meaning. Liberal means decades, not a year or two.

People care little and can't remember much about any brand. With skill and luck, advertisers may make one thing memorable. That's why it's critical in the beginning to be sure that the message is relevant to consumers.

When advertisers are unsure of their message, they fall for production techniques and gimmicks. Gimmicks wear out, the advertising gets junked and they start all over again, usually with a new message.

In some categories, brand parity is such that no relevant differentiation is possible. That does not change the need for consistency. Prudential has been "solid as the Rock of Gibraltar" for your entire life.

A meaningful message has an indefinite life. If advertisers err, it should be changing advertising too seldom, not too often. When they change, it should only be to present the same message in a new way.

It is up to the advertiser to maintain discipline. Agency creative people come and go. None wants to say what one before him said. It's up to the advertiser to see that he does.

As that infernal pink bunny, just "keep on going and going and going."

91 | Don't knock a good thing or change a successful ad.

If you read *The Wall Street Journal*, you've seen Lloyd Lane's advertising. You wouldn't call Lloyd a Madison Avenue guru. He's much better than that.

Yet Lloyd doesn't make his living making advertising. Lloyd makes his living because he knows how to make advertising for his own business. Lloyd has one smart client.

Lloyd Lane's advertising is contrary to what most advertisers want and most advertising makers want to make. Lloyd has only one ad. He runs it over and over again, year after year. The ad is small. It has no clever headline. It has very long copy in small type, with no photo or illustration.

The headline is "COLORADO VACATION" spread across two columns, in type not quite as high as the nail on your little finger. Beneath are 400 words of type two sizes smaller than you are reading now. The ad is 4 1/2 inches deep.

Lloyd owns what the ad describes as, "a small mountain resort for 80 guests and 45 staff." Copy includes everything about the location and lists everything anybody can do at Lloyd's resort. It includes what Lloyd's going to feed you, all about the evening entertainment, including the ragtime piano, what to do with your kids and how much it costs.

After 400 words, there's nothing left that you need to know about Lloyd's place. You can call, write or e-mail him for a reservation. If you call, Lloyd'll answer the phone.

The ad runs in all three editions of the *Journal* about 20 to 25 times a year in January, February, and March. Dozens of other resorts come and go as *Journal* advertisers. None is in Lloyd's league for advertising effectiveness.

Lloyd Lane is successful because he has a product people want. So in his ad's headline, he says nothing to draw attention away from the simple identity of that product.

He understands that to people who are interested in a Colorado vacation, you can't say too much.

It's the same about Nissans and Maytags and restaurants and whatever business you're in. If folks are interested, you just can't tell 'em too much. If they aren't, nothing at all matters.

Most advertisers make too many ads. Almost none make too few.

How long have you been advertising in the *Journal*, Lloyd?

"Forty years."

Ever thought about changing your ad?

"I added a couple inches to the bottom about 20 years ago when I had more to say."

How about a creative advertising agency with some fresh, new ideas, Lloyd?

"What for?"

92 | Brand advertising and retail advertising have little in common.

How can one of America's best retailers team up with one of the country's most creative advertising agencies with a bad result?

The agency, Fallon-McElligott, thought the client, McDonald's, should *build a brand image* for McDonald's new adult sandwich, Arch Deluxe. McDonald's really wanted to sell a lot more Arch Deluxes *right away*. The two objectives are not the same.

Only months after breaking Fallon-McElligott's campaign, McDonald's brought in two other agencies to make new Arch Deluxe commercials. Fallon's reputation couldn't suffer such a blow, so it resigned the $75 million Arch Deluxe assignment.

The problem stemmed from failure to heed a basic principle of advertising. There is a difference between creating advertising to sell merchandise today and creating advertising to build a brand.

McDonald's was already a powerful brand, but it is a retailer that is dependent upon daily sales. Fallon was an agency renowned for its brand building (BMW, Lee jeans, Nikon and Timex), but not for sell-it-today retail advertising.

In a *Wall Street Journal* interview, Fallon's president, Mark Goldstein, said, "Within nine days after they (the Fallon commercials) aired, 90% of Americans knew that McDonald's had a new burger for grownups," Goldstein said. That's real awareness, but awareness alone wasn't the issue.

It is difficult to criticize McDonald's effort to segment the already price-segmented hamburger market. Yet one hamburger for adults and another for children probably was a questionable segmentation strategy.

Though, McDonald's decision to build so-called adult burgers is not really the point. The crux of this matter is that Fallon made the wrong advertising for Arch Deluxe. Not bad advertising, *the wrong advertising*.

Making the wrong advertising is not uncommon. For years, Baskin Robbins advertised as though it were a brand of ice cream, which, of course, it is. In reality, though, to customers, Baskin Robbins is in the ice cream parlor retail business. There's a monumental difference.

Fallon-McElligott's experience and repeated success were in creating brand images for products sold in somebody else's stores. The agency had little experience in advertising for high turnover retail clients.

That is not Fallon's fault. It is McDonald's. If you hire a cow you will get milk, cream, maybe cheese, but not eggs. If you want eggs, you must hire a chicken or a turkey or a mocking bird.

Likewise, if you want to build a brand, hire a Fallon-McElligott. If you want advertising to induce people to try a new product today, right now in your already well-known stores, you must hire a firm that makes compelling retail advertising.

93 | Don't ask the football coach to lead the drama club.

You probably think you've had some boring days. You don't know boring until you spend two days judging an advertising contest.

Imagine an entire day watching and listening to nothing but local television and radio commercials and another day examining brochures, billboard photos, direct mail, newspaper and magazine ads.

You constantly have to remind yourself that somebody thinks each one is great. Somebody paid to produce each. Then somebody paid again to enter it in the contest.

The local radio advertising category always is the worst. There is nothing that compares to listening to several hundred bad radio commercials. Bad because they have one weakness in common. They are third-rate attempts at radio drama or comedy without professional actors or comedians.

If you have the services of fine radio actors, you can write 60-second dramas. If you have professional comedians, you can create truly funny radio commercials that benefit the brand and to which people will listen.

The problem is that these great acting voices and comedians don't exist in Fort Smith, Miami, Keokuk or Memphis. They live in Hollywood or New York, and they don't work cheap. In some cases, they won't work at all unless they like the script.

Their costs aren't outrageous. For locally aired commercials a great voice can be rented for less than $1,000. But local advertisers won't spend a few thousand dollars to create radio commercials.

Instead, they use local station announcers who cost less. That would be OK if local advertisers or their agencies would write 60-second announcements. Announcements are what announcers do well. And almost every market in America has some good announcers.

Additionally, local announcers have their own personalities in their markets. These announcers can play-act any role they want, but still the listener says, "Oh, that's so-and-so playing a forklift truck driver."

Whom is the advertiser trying to kid? The role of the forklift truck driver has no credibility.

This is one of the reasons why television stations do not allow on-air news staff members to make commercials. Station managers obviously believe their news people can not be credible journalists one minute and salesmen the next.

Local personalities can make commercials that are very effective, but only if the writers write copy that does not cast them in roles that stretch their credibility.

To get great commercial radio "theatre," you have to have great voice *actors*. If you won't pay the dough for actors, you'd better not let your advertising writer write scripts that require acting.

Actors act. Announcers announce.

94 | In print advertising frequently less is more.

It's great to be big.

Especially if you want to play basketball, or if you want to advertise in magazines or newspapers. Nobody argues that it's better to be able to afford a full-page than a small ad.

Yet many smaller, faster athletes are quite effective, and lots of advertisers are very successful with small, much less expensive ads.

Many advertisers believe that if they can't afford big ads, they shouldn't advertise in newspapers at all. Yet in most major cities, the only way an advertiser can reach a half-million people for a few hundred dollars is with a small ad in a daily newspaper.

In return on investment, small ads properly created can be more successful than large ads.

Advertisers think small ads won't be seen, and most aren't. Not because they're small, but because they are small versions of big ads.

Since they pay for every line of space, advertisers want to fill every line. They cram in everything they can. This makes ads cluttered and messy with no focus.

By sticking to three fundamentals, anyone can create successful, small newspaper ads. 1.) Say or show only one thing. 2.) Surround it with blank space. 3.) Write a headline of only one or two words. No more.

Advertisers who do these things make small ads that are interruptive and cost efficient. Two such advertisers are a financial planning outfit and a Buick dealer.

The financial guys run a one-column-by-two-inch ad in a local business journal. The headline is "Retired." The ad relates in 67 words a spoof of a mythical, 37-year-old client for whom the company has done such a good job that he has retired to Maui.

The Buick dealer runs ads of about 16% of a page in the daily newspaper that feature usually only one car and one price.

The secret of the car ads is a hefty use of blank space that makes them stand out. Much smaller, the financial ad uses liberal space between each line of copy to give an illusion of blank space.

The financial ad makes one sales point with an engaging, three-sentence benefit story. The Buick ads make one strong point and use blank space as a bold, clean statement to "own" any page on which they appear.

Effective, small newspaper and magazine ads require discipline. If you want to say two or three things, make two or three ads and alternate them.

Small ads are the classic example of "less is more." Less content and less money can beget more results.

95 | 'You gotta let them hogs know you got something for 'em.'

You've seen them on bumpers a thousand times. Stickers to "Support the Jaycees," "Support local schools." Support, support, support.

You get a compelling urge to run up and hammer on the guy's window yelling, "How? How? Tell me what to do?"

Non-profits, especially, but even many for-profit outfits, have a propensity to promote themselves in terms so unspecific that it is impossible to respond specifically. Unless people respond with some specificity, no response is worth much.

Compare "Support the church of your choice," for instance, with "Go to church" or even "Honk if you love Jesus." Compare "Support the SPCA" with "Spay your cat."

Going, honking, and spaying are actions you can take. "Support" ranks right up there with "We're a full-service bank," whatever that means.

The benefit of mass communication for advocacy is that it is a cheaper way to get action than sending salesmen to call one-on-one. It is difficult to recall any salesman including a plea for "support."

"Wellness" is a term in high vogue. Many spas promote wellness. What they're selling is a running track, swimming hole, exercise contraptions and weightlifting machines. They promote wellness because they say all good salesmen sell the benefit.

Well, there is wellness benefit also in running around your house or sticking your feet under the bed and doing sit-ups. Neither costs a couple-hundred bucks a month.

If you don't romance the hardware, you may create the "wellest" town in America without selling one membership.

In a small town nearby, there were once three banks. A papa bank, a mama bank and a wee, baby bank. The papa and mama banks advertised boastfully and un-specifically of the best bank service in town.

The baby bank advertising had no reference to service. Rather, the ads, themselves, served. One compared specific costs of financing a car through the bank vs. a car dealer. Another showed six different ways to finance a college education, including a bank loan.

These ads got action. Soon the baby bank was larger than the mama bank.

Maybe it's all the say-nothing political advertising that has led to a belief that consumers don't care about facts, just style. Yet specific response requires specific messages that call for specific action.

This is not to say that creativity and style are unimportant. It requires the greatest discipline to be specific with creativity and style. Being ignored is no more beneficial than being fuzzy.

As Fred Petzel, the 1929 hog calling champion of Iowa, said, "There must be power and appeal in your voice. You gotta let them hogs know you got somethin' for 'em."

96 | Look at it as a 48-foot can of beer, not a beer sign.

In 2001, in the U.S., advertisers wasted the better part of $3 billion on 406,000 billboards, because you couldn't read most of them.

Forget for a minute that billboards are a curse on the landscape. Concentrate instead on the waste of advertising dollars on billboards that are designed like the telephone Yellow Pages with almost as many words as the white pages.

Billboard advertising appeals to several business categories for obvious reasons. On the basis of cost-per-thousand-exposures, billboards are cheap. From about $1-to-$4-per-thousand-exposures, depending upon size and location. That's below the cost-per-thousand of other mass media.

Billboards are directional. They can advertise a hotel or restaurant at the next exit or nearby. That's why hotels and resorts comprise the No. 2 user category of billboards.

A great advantage of billboards is size. They are bigger than life. A so-called bulletin, those big billboards on the interstate system, allows an advertiser to exhibit his product as large as 14-by-48-feet. A billboard turned into a 48-foot can of beer is socko.

Yet when several elements are applied to one billboard, none has any impact, and the combination of elements reduces the billboard to just another roadside blur.

Billboards used properly can be very effective. If you can get beyond the urge to bulldoze them all, the issue is that not one out of 20 billboards is written or designed with any chance of being effective.

Average exposure time to an interstate bulletin-size billboard is two or three seconds. Maybe less in city traffic. The eye can get only a snapshot of any billboard, and the brain has to interpret that snapshot in those two or three seconds. Most Americans read at a sixth-to-eighth-grade level.

It is puzzling why billboard designers and buyers can't figure that out.

Billboard buyers judge a billboard design by holding in their hands an artist's layout about 18 inches long on a piece of art board. That's about three percent the size of a 48-foot billboard.

To judge the impact and readability of the 18-inch layout, it should be viewed from a distance that is about three percent of the distance from which motorists will view the billboard.

So, if a motorist will see your billboard from 200 yards away, you need to judge the layout from about six yards, or 18 feet, away. If every billboard buyer did that, he wouldn't buy billboard designs that nobody can read.

It should be a simple product illustration or logo and about three to five words BIG. No more.

97 | Who says there's no magic in advertising? 'Got Milk?'

A poll of brands with huge advertising budgets in 2002 indicated that marketers were losing faith in the power of advertising. So what else is new?

Every time the economy hits a speed bump, advertisers move dough out of advertising and into retail sales promotions and direct response activities.

This particular poll may be the result of other factors also. For instance, advertising dollars are less cost-efficient today because of media splintering in the last 20 years. Also, most campaigns in major media for several years have amounted to advertising road-kill.

Yet when brands have the benefit of razor-sharp strategies, accompanied by great advertising, remarkable things still happen.

If you don't believe there still is economic magic in advertising, then please explain, "Got Milk?"

In the beginning, there were only water and milk. For thousands of years milk's share of stomach decreased. In 1993, the California Milk Processor Board crafted a smart strategy, and its advertising agency created a great advertising campaign.

Consumer research focused the milk board's attention on how and when milk is most appealing to people. While soda pop may be preferred with salty snacks, people think milk goes better with sweet snacks, and nobody pours Pepsi on corn flakes.

So milk was advertised in partnerships with breakfast cereal, Oreo cookies, Entenmann's cakes and such.

"Got Milk?" advertising, including milk-mustachioed celebrities, has changed adolescents' image of milk. Instead of the traditional, medicinal, "Drink your milk; it's good for you," milk was repositioned as cool.

Milk now is desirable for the first time to an important market segment. Thus, this advertising has added value to milk.

It's what great brand advertising does.

Retail advertising's job is to deliver information. The primary role of brand advertising is to add value.

The California milk campaign quickly spread nationally, and a history of declining sales was reversed. Milk consumption increased for the first time in decades.

A declining economy always weeds out ineffective advertising. Brands that waste tens of millions on egocentric, obscure, misdirected, or otherwise worthless, advertising in good times pull in their horns when business slips.

Regardless of any current opinion poll, advertising remains the foundation for communicating a big idea.

It's not likely that the decision-makers at America's milk boards, AFLAC Insurance, Dell Computers or MasterCard have lost faith in the power of advertising. These brands get the advertising they're paying for.

Advertising remains the messenger that absolutely, positively adds value to brands when the message is on target. If the message is flawed, don't shoot the messenger.

PART TEN

SALES PROMOTION
Details. Details. Details.
Execution. Execution. Execution.

98 | Buzz, buzz, buzz may reap more than spend, spend, spend.

Advertising has reached the tipping point. Consumers have learned to tune it out. A new tactic is increasing in favor.

For more than 100 years, it was labeled "publicity stunt." For the past 30 years, it was called, "guerrilla marketing." Today, it is known simply as "buzz."

Buzz grabs the attention and imagination of blasé consumers, and it's affordable.

Buzz is promotional activity. It may be bold and audacious, a juxtaposition of elements or location. It may be packaging innovation, or veiled commercial messages delivered as news. Buzz often involves humor. Buzz may be created even in advertising.

Buzz is designed to turn consumers themselves into a medium that delivers the promotional message to other consumers, as in "buzz, buzz, buzz."

Swiss Swatch Watches were introduced in Germany by a 500-foot watch suspended from the top of the tallest skyscraper in Hamburg. An auto body shop owner printed refrigerator magnets to look like band aids, with "Ouch" and the shop's name and address. He hired kids to slap them on cars with dented fenders.

A marinade maker hired 20-somethings to tie tin cans behind their cars and paint "Just Marinaded" and the brand name on the trunks.

Pharmaceutical companies hire star athletes to talk about their ailments on radio and TV talk shows and name the medicines they use. A law firm put its name, phone number and "Personal Injury Attorneys" on yellow, plastic barriers and placed them on broken sidewalks and wet floors.

This is buzz, where innovation and clever thinking replace dollars.

With some products, buzz just happens. The Harry Potter books are so engaging that it would have been impossible to suppress the buzz.

That's the exception. Most successful buzz campaigns are carefully conceived and executed by highly experienced pros. The VW retro-Beetle was conceived to create buzz for Volkswagen's entire line. The Beanie Baby craze was pure, unadulterated buzz.

Tickle Me Elmo became a Christmas blockbuster in 1996 because a public relations agency sent one to Rosie O'Donnell's son, and Rosie played with the doll on her show, setting off a publicity mushroom.

The Goodyear and Snoopy blimps are buzz tactics. The guy who used to dress up as Mr. Peanut and hand out free peanuts in front of the Planters Peanut store was buzz.

Every brand can use buzz as a cost-efficient and effective promotional tactic. Success requires imagination, discipline and a lot of picky follow-through.

Ever wonder who to credit for those huge, white H-O-L-L-Y-W-O-O-D letters you've seen a million times? Call him "Buzz."

99 | Tote the biggest drum or skip the parade.

Only government is growing faster than commercial sponsorship of previously non-commercial buildings and events.

There's not a major arena in the U.S. without multi-million-dollar identity of some brand. Title sponsorship is a critical element in the financing of any arena or event.

In most cases, sponsors don't get much for their money, because they don't know how to get their money's worth, or they don't make the effort. If it's merely to help some charity, fine. Give to the ones you like. Tell the others, "No."

If sponsor participation is intended to provide some promotional benefit for the company, it's more complex.

The Wall Street Journal reported that a survey after one recent Olympics showed that companies that did not pay to be Official Olympics Sponsors were identified as sponsors by more Americans than some of the companies that paid up to $40 million to be sponsors.

The most important rule is to gain identity. The president of McDonald's once told his assembled franchisees, "March only in parades in which McDonald's has the biggest drum."

Too many companies fritter away a lot of money two-bits at a time. To get the loudest drumbeat you have to limit participation to events that you can dominate.

Only *title* sponsorship is worth much. Don't spend money to be in "other sponsors." If it's not the Acme Marathon, Acme Fiesta or the Acme Concert you won't get much identity for your dough.

Select opportunities that match your target customer. Don't promote a sports car at a quilting contest. Adopt a successful event, or choose a newcomer with potential. Get in bed only with organizations that have successful histories, legacies of sound leadership.

Then slap your name as big as you can on the biggest drum. Fight for the elimination of other sponsor names on the drum before you sign up. Check every detail. When John Hancock Insurance sponsored the Boston Marathon, it made sure that race organizers re-routed the finish line away from the entrance to the Prudential Life Building.

Follow your dough with elbow grease. Help promote the event. Get involved in every facet, and push hard. Involve company employees and customers. Milk your sponsorship until your pail runneth over.

As traditional advertising clutter continues to worsen, more companies are searching for promotional opportunities that differentiate them. If you're in the book business, sponsor the spelling bee. If you sell running shoes, sponsor something with many feet running.

Pick a solid organization, a solid event or one with potential, build the biggest drum and beat it loudly.

100 | Two can tango if you pick the right partner.

"Relationship marketing," cooperative promotion between two brands, is as old as the hills, but it's gotten some interesting new twists.

When two brands got together years ago for a joint promotion, it was usually to stretch advertising and promotion dollars. "You ante up $1 million for your crackers. I'll match it for my peanut butter, and each one of us will get a $2 million bang."

This kind of relationship marketing still occurs, but there are newer approaches to the concept that revolve around factors other than just pooling promotional dollars of two or more brands.

On a Northwest Airlines flight out of Memphis, you may be served a Corky's Barbecue, and it'll be identified as Corky's. Hundreds of millions of mail-order catalogs every year are loaded with FedEx logos and recommendations for customers to select FedEx shipping.

Another new twist in relationships has been a combination of food suppliers and restaurants. Subway featured an A.1. Steak and Cheese Sandwich with a bottle of A.1. Steak Sauce in the TV commercial.

An even more interesting technique has been a relationship that places a brand in a totally new promotional venue, away from its competitors, to target specific market segments.

To reach BMW and Lexus buyers in behalf of its Cirrus model, Chrysler partnered with Brooks Bros., Frank Lloyd Wright landmarks and Ticketmaster to isolate prospects where they buy clothes and concert tickets and tour landmarks.

Cirrus was advertised in the Brooks Bros. catalogs and via display materials in Brooks Bros. stores, at landmarks of the famous architect and in Ticketmaster envelope stuffers for just the right concerts.

While expensive on a cost-per-thousand-impressions basis, it was a relatively low-cost strategy to reach the target market in fresh, unexpected and uncluttered venues.

There is hardly a category or brand that could not benefit from such a relationship marketing strategy. It takes a massive logistical effort, but the cost and potential are attractive.

The key element is compatibility. Compatible geography, because a national brand usually won't partner with a regional brand. Compatible customer demographics; BMW wouldn't welcome a tie-in with Wal-Mart. Compatible timing; Paas Easter Egg Dyes and Christmas wrap are a mismatch.

The initiating partner brings found-money to the pocket of the passive partner in the relationship. A Chrysler display on the floor is not offensive to the Brothers Brooks, and the display fee is money in the Brooks pocket.

Grab a compatible partner that offers a fresh venue, one where your best prospects gather and away from influences that compete with your brand.

101 | Targeted promotions can fall on the wrong eyes and ears.

There was a time when politicians got away with promising one thing on one side of town and another on the other side, and when brands could advertise and promote to a specific market segment without other segments knowing.

Neither remains a possibility. The media is so pervasive today that no brand can promote to any group without everybody else getting wind of what it's doing.

Thus, today's politically correct speech fetish, litigants under every rock and people who are offended by the most innocent comment make it critical that any advertising and promotional scheme is considered very carefully.

You read about the so-called radio "shock-jocks" in New York who were fired for broadcasting a purportedly live account of two people having sex in New York's St. Patrick's Cathedral.

You may not have heard of the repercussions against Samuel Adams Beer.

The incident was part of WNEW-FM's "Sex for Sam" contest. Entrants were to have sex in public places for prizes that included trips to concerts sponsored by Sam Adams Beer.

To compound the promotional grievance, the chairman of the brewery, Jim Koch, was in the studio and on the show during the dastardly deed.

The result, as you would expect, was outrage. Worse for Mr. Koch, it included a boycott of Sam Adams Beer by bartenders in its home market of Boston.

Although an extreme example, it demonstrates the dangers that brands risk in all advertising and promotion.

You may launch a promotion designed for a specific target market to which your scheme is not offensive. When news of your shenanigans reaches other market segments, they have different opinions.

In an effort to help the Memphis Park Commission some years ago, Seessel's Supermarkets sponsored a Halloween party for kids on Mud Island.

When the event was publicized, people called to vilify Art Seessel for "sponsoring a Pagan event."

In 2001, Pepsi yanked a rapper television commercial after ultra-conservative Bill O'Reilly of Fox News attacked the rapper's sexually explicit lyrics and urged consumers to call the company.

If there's even the slightest chance that something might offend somebody, today you can be sure it will.

Large brands spend a lot of money on research to test advertising and promotional ideas beforehand. Small companies can't afford such.

If you're faced with these decisions, run the idea by as many people as possible. If you decide to do something controversial, at least you ought to know in advance from whom you'll get angry calls.

Remember. A lot of people are offended by the Pledge of Allegiance.

102 | Before you add a loyalty program, count your frequent flyer cards.

With a decline of brand loyalty among customers and the redefinition of a satisfied customer, no marketing tactic has been hotter the last 10 years than so-called customer-loyalty programs.

Most business travelers belong to three or four frequent flyer programs and as many hotel brand programs. Grocery shoppers carry two or three supermarket-brand loyalty cards in their wallets.

That's loyalty for you.

Every business category from soda pop to restaurants is offering, or has offered, some kind of loyalty or frequency-marketing promotion. All are expensive to operate and communicate. Most accomplish little or nothing for the brand.

Loyalty marketing specialists know that consumers aren't fools. If the program rewards aren't worth much, nobody takes part. If rewards are meaningful, they become very expensive for the provider. The airlines are saddled with the liability of trillions of frequent-flyer miles.

Loyalty programs also can backfire and create animosity among customers. When an airline increases the number of miles required for a free ticket, it devalues the customer's mileage.

Even worse, programs often deny customer benefits if they don't pay full price. In a recent stay in the Radisson Hotel at the

Cincinnati airport, the clerk said that Radisson Club points couldn't be awarded, because the room rate was too low to justify points.

You either have a loyalty program or you don't. If you give 150 points for a $150 room, you have to give 50 points for a $50 room.

One problem with most loyalty programs is that they are conceived poorly. All contingencies and possibilities are not considered up front. They either prove to be too costly, in which case benefits later must be reduced, or benefits are inadequate to accomplish the program's objectives.

The greatest problem with almost all loyalty programs, though, is that they are created in a vacuum, then duplicated too easily by competitors.

A Memphian going to Atlanta may choose Northwest Airlines, because, with a Northwest hub in Memphis, she can earn a free ticket sooner. An Atlantan coming to Memphis may choose Delta Airlines, because Atlanta is a Delta hub.

Chances are, though, both flyers belong to both frequent flyer programs and may choose their airline based on flight times. The frequent user programs of all major airlines and lodging chains, virtually, are comparable.

If your company's thinking about a loyalty program, be sure it's attractive enough to entice customers, that you know what it'll cost and that the competition can't duplicate it overnight. Otherwise, you'll have the costs without any benefit.

103 | Better have the lowest cost before you cut the price.

The most popular tactic to increase sales and market share quickly is to cut prices. If you know that you have lower operating costs than competition, cut deep, lay it on 'em and drive them out of business. The sooner the better.

On the other hand, price-cutting is misunderstood, misused and hurts the price-cutter more often than it hurts competition.

When Coke six-packs are 99 cents at Kroger, it usually means that Pepsis are 99 cents at Wal-Mart. Retailers benefit from a popular price leader that may increase traffic. Consumers save dough. Virtually no benefits accrue to Coke and Pepsi.

Price cuts may change Coke and Pepsi market shares a fraction briefly but have no effect on long-term shares.

Consumers stock up on their favorite brands when they're on special. Some may switch brands if another is on special. The presumption is that some switchers will drink a six-pack and change preference to that brand at higher prices in the future. Fat chance.

These tactics keep a thumb on the lesser brands, of course, but the principal result for Coke and Pepsi is a reduction in margins and profits with no real customer gains at higher margins later.

Why do they continue to do it? Retailers demand it. If Coke and Pepsi got together and bowed their necks, retailers would just sue them.

The same thing occurs in hamburgers. McDonald's, Burger King and Wendy's gain little from price-cutting. It only slashes franchisee margins.

This is true in soda pop and hamburgers because both categories are very mature. There breathes hardly a user in either category who has not sampled all brands and developed a preference.

So when is price-cutting effective?

When a new brand enters any category, it needs trial. Price-cutting is a proven tactic to gain trial that may build a permanent customer base for something genuinely new.

The same is true of volatile product categories and retail neighborhoods. If the product category or retail neighborhood is such that the customer mix is constantly churning, periodic price-cutting can create new customers.

The other primary benefit of cutting prices is to turn old or distressed merchandise into cash. If this is not your objective, if you don't have lower operating costs or if you can not gain new customers who will buy at higher prices later, price-cutting probably won't be profitable.

Never cut prices without analyzing carefully how competitors will respond. You may be better off with today's market share and margins than more or equal volume with lower margins.

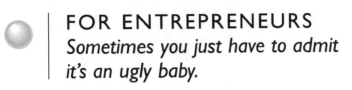

PART ELEVEN

FOR ENTREPRENEURS
Sometimes you just have to admit it's an ugly baby.

104 | Is this a business? That is the question.

Probably at least once in your career you've thought about starting your own company. If you have achieved any measure of success and self-confidence by your 30s, you've toyed with the idea.

Nowadays, there's help for anybody with the urge. There are seminars of all kinds about starting new businesses. There are consultants, accountants, bankers, even retired executive groups that will help.

You can learn the basic needs and pitfalls of a startup, all the reasons why new businesses fail. If your idea is not unique, say just another hamburger joint or car repair shop, that kind of information may be all you need.

Yet if your idea is not already a category in the Yellow Pages, if it's a new concept, that kind of information is not enough. The big question is, "Is this a business?"

Melba Duncan had to ask that question.

Duncan was a world class executive assistant for a Wall Street CEO. She knew there are more than 1,500 search firms that recruit high-level executives. Today, there's no more likelihood of an undiscovered, star CEO than of an undiscovered 17-year-old lefthander who can throw 95 mph.

Not so with executive assistants. To find a great one, execs skulk around and try to steal one. Many asked Melba Duncan where they could find her clone.

That's when Duncan knew, according to her account in *Inc. Magazine*, "This is a business." So she opened the Duncan Group, Inc. Fourteen years later it still was the only search firm dealing exclusively in locating executive assistants.

She was wise enough not to trust just her own instinct. She exposed her idea to a list of top executives. The final test was what her boss, the CEO of his own startup, thought of her idea.

He thought so much of it that he swallowed the thought of losing her, lent her $30,000 to start and introduced her to an experienced executive searcher who advised Duncan, then became her No. 1 stockholder.

A fresh, new business idea is frail. It's your child. You don't want to hear bad things. You shield it from attack, so you're not willing to test it on smart people. You can't bear anybody poking holes in it.

Yet that's the true test of whether your idea can be a business. Will people pay money for it? How much? Why won't it work? You must ask as many successful people as you can, even if you have to pay them to listen.

If any wants to invest, it's probably a business.

105 | Starting a new business? You already have decades of brand equity.

In 1967, a young man who was thinking about opening an advertising agency told his wife, "I think I'll call it Mid-South Advertising," to which she said, "You're nuts."

"Mid-South Advertising doesn't mean anything. The only people who are going to do business with you are those who know you. Call it John Malmo Advertising."

Of course, she was right. That name served the agency successfully for 25 years.

In the 36 years since that conversation, many other individuals have gone into free-lancing or their own personal services businesses without the benefit of Betty Malmo. They made a big mistake.

A couple names that come to mind are Indelible Inc and Design Takeout.

Indelible Inc is the business name for a professional writer who has worked for well-known firms in her market. For that, and her active participation in the local advertising federation, she is well known in advertising circles.

Design Takeout is the business name for a talented young graphic designer who is also well known among local advertising people in her market.

Both of these business names are clever. The problem is that, as in the case of "Mid-South Advertising," they don't mean anything. Yet the names and reputations of these two young women mean a lot to potential customers.

This matter of misidentifying individual, personal services businesses is not restricted to advertising. Many individuals and partners have gone into business to offer information technology services and have contrived kicky-sounding technical names for their businesses.

We make these mistakes because we think it sounds more important to have an impersonal business identity than to use our own names. Boy, we sure don't want people to think it's just me, or just the two of us.

Invariably, entrepreneurs make the mistake of believing that they should sound bigger than they are. The opposite is true.

In the first place, you don't fool anybody. You blow your cover when they call you and hear the baby crying or realize your home address matches your business address.

More important, everyone admires entrepreneurs. The primary appeal of hiring a very small firm is that you get to work with the owner. The owner, himself, does the work you ordered.

Besides, friends and customers can remember your name, but not that funky name you gave yourself.

If you're striking out on your own in a personal services business, take advantage of your No. 1 asset, your own reputation and contacts. Name the business after you. You already have 30 or 40 years equity in that brand.

106 | Pay the business first and yourself second.

There are lots of truisms that apply to opening a new business.

One is, "Lose money the first year, break even the second and make money the third year. If you can last three years, the business probably will make it." Maybe so.

A lot truer, though, is this one. "Most new businesses fail from a lack of capital." That's a fact, according to the Department of Commerce.

There must be a book of substantial reasons for cash starvation, many of which a startup owner may not be able to control.

There is one that causes startup failure, though, over which every entrepreneur has control. That is how much money he or she or they take out of the business for himself, herself or themselves.

Many new businesses fail because a little early success goes too fast to the owner's head and hip. If a startup business has the good fortune to open on a financial track of black ink, it is a euphoric feeling. The disciplinary pain required to keep from taking home the spoils is excruciating.

The temptation is strong to believe that surely the sky is the only limit. To sober up, you have only to drive through shopping centers and business parks counting the "for sub-lease" and "going out of business" signs.

In any business, the owner has to realize in the beginning that it is the business, not he or she, that must come first.

Capital accumulation is the most critical next step after any early business success to assure the continuation of that success. That comes from feeding the business better than you feed yourself.

It's always easy to learn to raise your standard of living. It's darn near impossible for most people to learn to live on less than that to which they have become accustomed.

Every entrepreneur should compute his minimum fixed living expenses, then draw a salary from the business that equals that amount.

Once the business is open, accrue all profits in the business to protect against a downturn. A wise entrepreneur will always pay himself a realistic salary that he believes he could earn from another employer in the event his business should fail.

This assures accumulation of capital, and she can always raise her standard of living once a cushion is built. If the business does fail and the erstwhile owner has to look elsewhere for employment, she will retain, at least, her current standard of living.

Further, she is less likely to have to recover personally from credit-and-reputation-damaging bankruptcy.

107 | Cash flow provides options. No cash flow, no options.

A highly competent public relations man with 25 years experience could not comprehend that resigning a client that was unprofitable on paper did not, necessarily, constitute a profitable decision.

"The account created $30,000 income," he said. "It cost us $40,000 in staff hours. By losing the account we have added $10,000 to our bottom line."

He didn't understand that the company now had $30,000 less income. Unless the company eliminated more than $30,000 in cash outflow, it was worse off.

Many talented business people don't have the foggiest notion about elementary aspects of business finances. Cash flow, what constitutes a profit, the cost of receivables are absolutely foreign to them.

Cash flow often is the most overlooked element, especially in small and start-up businesses. It's a truism that most companies' problems could be solved by greater cash flow.

If a company is creating enough income, management has many options to turn some of that income into profit. The more cash it generates, the easier it is to manage the business.

When a company's cash flow is inadequate, managers have no options. They must cut expenses fast. Compounding the problem is that, if you cut the people you can most easily do without, you don't reduce expenses much. To cut personnel expenses appreciably, you have to cut high-priced people, the ones you need to rebuild cash flow.

Take the lost $30,000 client. If you keep the 30 grand, you can try to manage people working on the account more efficiently, improve productivity and decrease the time required. You might place lower-cost people on the business.

The fact is that most businesses are at their profit peak when everybody is overworked and the company is understaffed. That assumes, of course, that employees are not paid a premium for overtime. Such is the case in most service businesses.

Do you add people to get new business or do you wait for new business to add the people? Unless the business has strong cash reserves, the answer is an emphatic, get the business first. Cash flow from most new business is overestimated during the chase and even if you win, it takes longer to develop income than you think.

After the business is in the house, you'll have a clearer picture of who you need and what you can pay them.

It is a fact that most start-up companies go belly-up for lack of money. Cost accounting is a wonderful tool, but running off business that you think is unprofitable simply may reduce your options before you've considered them.

| 108 | If you don't see opportunity, you aren't looking hard enough. |

Surely the most wonderful thing about capitalism is that it gives people opportunities. Opportunities to try anything they want, no matter how screwy it sounds. The opportunity to succeed and, conversely, to fail is an equally important element in the equation.

Think of the exciting things that have been going on in capitalist societies in just the last couple decades. The giant progress in computer and communications technology, medicine, every category of consumer goods.

From computer chips to mail-order gazebos, Aunt Lizzie's Cheese Straws and second-hand hubcaps, innovation comes from capitalism. It's impossible to name one significant innovation that's come from non-capitalist systems in the same period.

Take the guy who processed broccoli. Every year he threw away 40 million pounds of broccoli stems. Then one day it occurred to him to grind up those stems and make cole slaw out of 'em.

He developed a multi-million-dollar slaw business. A government broccoli operation would still be littering landfills with broccoli stems.

In the back of *Fortune* magazine you see an ad to call 1-800-ELEPHANT for the Elephant Secretary. It's a greeting card service. Pick out your cards and fill out a form with the dates, names and addresses of birthdays, anniversaries and such that you want to remember.

They even scan your handwriting and send the cards with your signature digitized. Now that's exciting.

Owner Douglas Jefferys was a motorcycle dealer. Then he went into the mail order gazebo business. Made 88 models of gazebos, from $2,000 to $77,000 each and sold them by mail. "All 385 Marriott Courtyards in America have one of my gazebos," he says.

He sold that company to his partner and started the elephant thing. In four years, he had 20,000 customers and predicted sales would top $1 million the fifth year.

A $5 million business in mail order gazebos, a $1 million business sending out greeting cards. Wow.

Then there's Aunt Lizzie's Cheese Straws. Two friends started making the spicy little devils in 1983. From her kitchen, Ginna Kelley says, they grew the company to mid-six figures in 10 years. Can a six figure cheese straw business be profitable? "Oh, yes, indeed," Kelley says.

America is alive with Hubcap Annies and Aunt Lizzies and guys who call themselves "Elephant Secretary." With all the opportunity and all the incentive, it's a shame that we don't teach capitalism more aggressively.

Just as Lee Trevino, the poor, little Mexican-American kid who made millions of dollars hitting a golf ball, says, "Is this a great country, or what?"

109 | Your eyes can get too big for your stomach.

The problem with taking your kids to a cafeteria is that everything looks so good to them that their eyes get too big for their tummies.

It happens to small business owners, too. Often, owners of small, growing businesses make the mistake of going after customers they're not ready to handle.

It's not unusual for an aggressive small fry to land a large customer that it lacks the capacity to absorb. Its resources get spread too thin, service declines to existing customers, and the small company plays catch-up every day with its new 800-pound gorilla.

Some existing customers get short-changed and jump ship. The big, new account rethinks its decision and departs, as well.

Perhaps the most perplexing issue that ever faces every entrepreneur at some point is the chicken-and-egg debate. Does he go after one big, new customer with his existing resources, hoping to add capacity if he gets the business, or does she roll the dice, add capacity beyond her current means and hope she gets the new business to pay for her higher overhead?

Sears used to have so-called "basic suppliers." These were manufacturers from which it bought goods on a cost-plus basis. Sears never wanted to be so important to any of them that Sears might suffer bad publicity from putting the company under if Sears were to move its business.

The American Association of Advertising Agencies tells small and medium-sized members never to allow any one account to amount to more than 25% of the agency's business.

The Sears policy and the AAAA recommendation are sound thinking in behalf of small companies.

Yet what does the small business owner do? Does he tell one client that it's growing too fast, to take the added business elsewhere? Of course not.

Wise owners reinvest the profits from that account into added capacity. They redouble their sales efforts to add additional customers that will cushion the impact in the event that the major customer is lost.

Growth by one dominant account, of course, can be a windfall. Even chasing an over-sized customer before a half-pint company is ready for it may prove successful. There are many cases in which such good fortune has turned small companies into giants.

There are many more cases, though, in which an overly optimistic sales policy has caused irreparable damage.

If you get, then lose, a huge customer before you're ready, you may never get another shot at it. Be careful not to let your eyes get too big for your stomach.

110 | When the passion wanes, the quality goes with it.

American business gives off signals that it is obsessed with quality. Or is it just the idea of quality?

We imported from Japan the concept of quality circles. Then came total quality management, then so-called one-on-one relationship marketing to improve service quality. For a decade, every new business book that wasn't about leadership was about quality.

If we have an American mania for quality, why is quality in such short supply? We lack a passion for quality.

Most companies approach quality as a raw material. For $9.99 you get a pinch of quality. Two pinches are $29.99.

To climb Mount Everest, you have to do more than get a map. A few hundred steps won't do it. You have to be committed to reach the top. Quality is reaching the top. It starts with a passion to get there.

Many people enter business with no clear definition of what quality means in that category. Their real objective is to make money. They are only as good as they have to be to make money.

You can't just establish quality standards. You must perform to those standards. Not some of the time, *every time.*

An executive of the very successful Houston's Restaurants was quoted as saying there is a supervisor in every Houston's kitchen who examines every order before it goes to a table. The supervisor is supposed to verify that it meets Houston's *standards of quality*. Then you hear that a customer sent his soup back twice because it was not hot. The third time it still was room temperature.

It's not an accident that chef-owned restaurants are often the best. Or that specialty stores owned by people who turned their hobbies into businesses are often the best. These people have a passion.

History's most famous marketing educator said that profit is not the objective of business. Huh? Rather, it is a by-product, he said. The objective, according to Harvard's Ted Levitt, is to create and keep a customer. If you do that consistently, profit will be a by-product.

Being best builds a reputation that attracts customers. Being best every time keeps them. Quality *performance*, not quality standards.

An electronics store with a brilliant stocking and merchandising plan can't be successful with a staff of clerks that knows little about the merchandise.

There is always room at the top of every category and little room anywhere else. Businesses perform with top quality when the person at the top has a passion to be the best. Being the best defines quality.

Index

Jack Daniels Whiskey, 176
Janitor in a Drum, 173
Jeep, 176
Jefferys, Douglas, 237
Jergens Lotion, 173
Jesus, 46, 206
JFK Airport, 41
Jimmy Dean Pork Sausage, 29
John Hancock Insurance, 217
John Malmo Advertising, Inc., xvi,
  230
Jolly Royal, 74
Journal of Pastoral Care, 46
Kaytee Products, 172
Keebler Cookies, 170
Kelley, Ginna, 237
KFC, 32, 76, 176
Kim, W. Chan, 108
Kimberly-Clark Corporation, 98, 99
Kleenex, 168
Klein, Calvin, 107
Kmart, 83, 122
Koch, Jim, 220, 221
Krispy Kreme Donuts, 113
Kroger, 76, 79, 83, 224
LaCoste, Rene, 174
Lane, Lloyd, 198, 199
Lauren, Ralph, 47
La-Z-Boy Recliners, 79, 157, 175,
  194, 195

LeBonheur Children's Medical
  Center, 56
Lee Jeans, 200
L'eggs, 29
Lenin, Vladimir, 68, 69
Lepper, Dr. Mark R., 144
Levitt, Theodore, 122, 123, 241
Lexus, 139, 219
Lincoln, 84
Linder, Lionel, xvii
Lionel Trains, 154, 155
Lipscomb, Ed, xv
Lite Beer, 196
Livingston, J. Sterling, 6, 7
London Fog, 44, 45
Louis Harris & Associates, 126
Loveman, Gary, 119
Low, Prescott, xiv
Malmo, Betty, 230
Marlboro Cigarettes, 45, 166, 196
Marriott Courtyard, 237
Martin, "Abbo," xiv
Martin, Chap, 180, 181
Marx, Karl, 48
MasterCard, 211
Mauborgne, Renee, 108
Maytag, 199
Maytag TurboChef, 111
McDonald's, xvi, 13, 16, 54, 66, 76,
  77, 84, 106, 107, 169, 200, 201,
  216, 225